The Politics of Faith

*Essays on the morality of
key current issues*

Peter C. Glover

Copyright © 2004 by Peter C. Glover

The Politics of Faith
by Peter C. Glover

Printed in the United States of America

ISBN 1-594677-96-4

All rights reserved solely by the author. The author guarantees all contents are original and do not infringe upon the legal rights of any other person or work. No part of this book may be reproduced in any form without the permission of the author. The views expressed in this book are not necessarily those of the publisher.

Unless otherwise indicated, Bible quotations are taken from The New King James Version of the Bible. Copyright © 1990, 1985, 1983 by Thomas Nelson, Inc.

www.xulonpress.com

Dedicated to those who live by reason – and who are wise enough to know that we also live by faith.

Always be ready to give a defense to everyone who asks you a reason for the hope that is in you.
I Peter 3:15.

THE POLITICS OF FAITH
Essays on the morality of key current issues

Preface ix

1. **Saddam & The Death Penalty** 13
   (ISSUES: the death penalty & the fate of Saddam Hussein)

2. **WAR & PEACE - The Pre-Emptive Strike:
   is it moral?** 35
   (ISSUES: self-defence & weapons of mass destruction)

3. **WAR & PEACE - The Invasion of Iraq:
   was it justified?** 47
   (ISSUES: the anatomy & morality of the war in Iraq)

4. **Who Killed David Kelly?** 69
   (ISSUES: media responsibility & suicide)

5. **The Liberal Bias of the Media** 77
   (ISSUES: values & politics in the media)

6. **Liberal & Conservative Thinking:** *just a political
   mindset or a whole way of reasoning?* 91
   (ISSUES: the battle for the mind & defending one's home)

7. **So What *Is* Your Worldview?** 107
   (ISSUE: identifying personal patterns of belief)

8. **The Limits of the Civil Law** 139
   (and its application in the spanking of children)
   (ISSUES: civil obedience & child discipline)

9. **When TV Gets the Morality Right** 147
   (ISSUE: media morality & abortion)

10. *(Observations on the controversies surrounding)*
    Mel Gibson's the Passion of the Christ 155
    (ISSUES: anti-Semitism & Christian evangelism)

11. **Why Are So Many Modern Christians *So* Gullible?** 175
    (ISSUE: the modern Christian mind)

12. **The Church in Cyberspace:** *Boldly going where no church has gone before?* 183
    (ISSUES: the nature of worship & who defines it)

Preface

When people speak of a 'moral' perspective, what they usually mean, in our predominantly postmodern world, is a personalized, often shifting, view of what is right and what is wrong. This book will approach some of the issues of the day from a very different perspective. It will adopt a thoroughly theistic worldview — one which dominated all Western political and social development until the last century.

It is my view that postmodern liberalism is inherently blind to its own chief failing. For postmodernism holds that everything is true, *except* the belief that absolute truth can be true absolutely. But it holds this particular exemption as true, *absolutely*. If the reader is closed to the notion that all philosophical systems, whether psychological or religious, are ultimately 'faith-based', then try postmodernism — but beware, you *will* need a great deal of faith.

That brings me to why I raise here the subject of 'politics' when it comes to 'faith'. The predominant philosophy of our age is almost certainly humanist and postmodern. In the wake of its success, conservative Christian theistic thinkers — the 'fathers' of modern science, of modern education and of modern liberal democracy (as any decent history of the last five hundred years will tell you) — have had a bad press. The fact that they rarely get a good press, is, we shall see, down to both the intolerance of liberal elites who increasingly deny them a voice, *and* a progressively incoherent church affected, as it is, by invasive 'religious' forms of postmodern thinking.

As a result of the former we have become used to receiving our news, education and popular (as opposed to real) science from sources which turn out to be far from 'value-less'. That is why I have put together these 12 essays and articles for both general and Christian consumption alike. They only cover a small area of that which could be reviewed. But my purpose here is to articulate something of how a biblical worldview has a great deal to say about, and to, the modern world. I am personally ashamed that the contemporary church, and especially its liberal leadership, is so disengaged from the surrounding culture that it has little to say to it. Christians either become infused with the worldly entertainment culture or disengaged in 'holier-than-thou' piety — both being paralysed into inactivity in the public arena. In short, the contemporary church is not doing its job by being 'salt' as well as 'light' in the world.

For that reason it is encumbent upon us all to review the validity of our particular worldview. And we can do this by examining questions such as: Should Saddam Hussein suffer the death penalty? Do we have the right to spank our children? Does suicide offer a 'better deal' than life? Is the news we receive daily into our living rooms really 'philosophy free'? And, even more prosaically, how can any of us speak of right and wrong when we have such different values?

This series of essays and articles has been written to show that logic and reason and morality and faith are far from being 'strange bedfellows'. I hope there is something here for everyone. Above all, it is my greatest desire that the plain speaking and reasoning adopted will challenge the myth of a world 'out of control' and 'without purpose'.

What drew me to a biblical worldview was not liberal politicking, nor blind faith, but the unshakeable higher logic of the Master of truth and wisdom himself, Jesus Christ. If politics is the 'science of government' and *all* systems of understanding are, ultimately, 'faith-based', we owe it to ourselves to explore the politics of our faith.

Peter C Glover
Summer 2004

ISSUES: The death penalty, the fate of Saddam
& the human rights agenda

1
Saddam & the Death Penalty

Whether it's Saddam Hussein facing the death penalty, the latest high-profile trial, or the fate of asylum seekers, we all hold an opinion. But it is less than wise, so it seems, to express that opinion publicly, especially in the media, if one wishes to avoid the clamorous censures of the liberal elites and lobbies. For them, the only 'acceptable' opinion on *any* morality issue is one that favours *individual* human rights above *communal* human rights. Let me explain.

Take the issue of smoking. The conservative thinker tends to the opinion that public area bans are perhaps appropriate in the interest of 'all'. For my own liberal baby boomer generation, however, still living out the vestiges of our 'let it all hang out' college days, the restriction of any personal freedoms, even for the sake of the majority, runs against the grain. Then there is the right to abortion on demand, euthanasia, the legalization of cannabis, the desire for designer babies, gay marriage et al. Even though most polls consistently reveal liberal opinion as a minority on most of these issues — the general population no doubt recognizing the community dimension — the liberal individualizing slant still dominates in the political arena and the media, especially TV and radio. Indeed, such is the worldview of most liberal commentators that barely an issue today escapes their reduction of it down to its narrowest human rights dimension — a dimension then expressed as if it were the 'commonly held view', rather than what it often is, a minority opinion.

We would do well to be far more alert to the frailties of the TV 'entertainment culture', where even hard news is presented as 30-second sound-bite 'infotainment'. As the late Neil Postman observed, TV so easily enables us to 'amuse ourselves to death'.[1] Liberal sound-bite invective makes for good TV. It can always be relied upon for cutting, moral-high-ground-sounding comment that, in the shallow world of TV culture, passes itself off as 'well-informed' and 'logical' — when it is neither.

Various media commentators, such as Neil Postman, Marshal McLuhan and others, have long observed that television is just not a good medium either for serious debate or for gaining an in-depth understanding of most issues. It is essentially a singularly one-dimensional medium, where all that we see and hear is governed by the decisions, whims and worldview of a faceless oligarchy. We would do well to recognize this. That is why, against all the odds, at the beginning of the twentieth century many of us still read broadsheet newspapers and books and, increasingly, receive information via the Internet. The advent of the latter, above all, will ensure — at least as long as it remains unregulated news-wise — information unfettered by the restrictive policies of an often liberal-dominated, politically correct, modern media.

I wonder if you have noted, for instance, how consistent liberal commentators on contemporary issues are successfully diverting almost every discussion affecting the broader community into an emotive bottom-line wrangling about individual human rights — and utilizing 'worst case scenario' examples to make their point? Which brings us neatly back to the current hot topic: whether Saddam Hussein should face the death penalty, and the predominant themes surfacing around the issue in the media. One can only wonder at how talk of the death penalty for those *guilty* of murder — which *must* at some level be in the interest of the wider community — can so easily animate liberal ire when, at the same time and by perverse logic, that ire is also animated in favour of aborting perfectly *innocent* young lives in the womb as if the matter of abortion has no community dimension, when it plainly does.[2] Historically, when it comes to the adoption of what George W. Bush has referred to as 'ultimate justice' (judicial execution), we note that our Western Judeo-Christian heritage has taken its lead from a biblical heritage and thereby God-given mandate that confirms human autonomy in performing judicial executions.[3] It is of course a penalty still available in allegedly anti-death penalty nations such as Britain, where it remains on the statute book for the crimes of treason and piracy on the high seas. Having said that, the prevailing liberal elite of the European Union have seen to it that membership of the EU is not even open to nations who practise the use of the death penalty.

Between television's trivializing of most issues and its thrusting forward of high profile liberals to reduce the argument, as is their wont, to the perennial discussion about human rights (and which of us does *not* care about these?), genuine well-informed and articulate opinion is, on TV and radio, becoming as elusive as a third runway at Heathrow or genuine security at American airports. But before we leave the subject, let us see just how the liberal-minded thought-police go about their business.

Within two days of the capture of Saddam Hussein, the media debate had been whipped into a lather by various activists demanding Saddam's human rights. But in the clamour for him to be tried by an international tribunal, liberals gave the game away — that they care little for the rights of the most relevant community, the Iraqi people, and more for their own private, human rights obsessed, agenda. And it does not take too much cerebral calibrating to work out why. If the death penalty can be morally right *in principle* for any human being, *even* a deposed and murderous presidential thug, it must also be right in principle in other cases too. And as such, Bush's 'ultimate justice' for Saddam Hussein could prove an unassailable moral precedent for the reintroduction of the death penalty more generally. *Ipso facto* the need is, in this most high profile of cases, to win the prevailing argument not to execute him and prevent a central principle of liberalism from receiving a mortal blow itself.

No wonder leading liberals were out in force after Saddam's capture! Even the liberal-dominated United Nations felt the need to restate its anti-death penalty credentials. Given the UN's capacity to have its policing troops stand idly by and do nothing to prevent mass murder, as a matter of policy, in places like Bosnia, Iraq and elsewhere, this is a little hard to swallow. But we must remember that what Kofi Annan was talking about were Saddam's human rights, not those of the Iraqi population. In his pontifications on the subject, neither did Annan address the issue of how Saddam's murderous hand could be stayed from ordering yet more murders from a future prison cell, as easily as from his palace in Bagdhad. But then the UN, like us all, is entitled to its opinion, is it not?

Inevitably the issue of Saddam and the death penalty has been the focus of attention around the world. While Saddam has now been handed over to the new post-war interim Iraq Government, there are still those who carp that he should been tried by an international tribunal. The main reason behind the carping, however, has little to do with grumbling over the potential fairness of the trial, but rather with the nature of the sentence he is likely to receive. The same human rights activists who were vocal that he ought to be tried by an international tribunal have now refocused their efforts on getting the UN and the international community to bring pressure to bear on the Iraqis to pass any sentence, except the death penalty. But, whether Saddam ultimately is incarcerated or dies a judicial death,[4] I would argue that the moral case for him to be tried by a purely Iraqi tribunal, which must be left to decide as it sees fit, is actually unarguable. After all, who has the greater right? Milosovic's crimes were not committed against his own Serbian people, but against the international community. Trying him in a Serbian court would have been highly inappropriate (even though we have had to suffer the excruciatingly long farce of the international trial itself which has already seen off its first judge and is in the throes currently of seeing off the defendant too). Saddam's murderous crimes, though committed against the international community in general, were committed *primarily* against his own people. The Iraqis thus must have first shout — the very last thing liberals want, since they know well enough that the penalty for murder, mass and otherwise, in Iraq, has usually been death. So the liberal campaign has concentrated on gathering a head of steam decrying the possibility of a fair trial in Iraq, especially before an 'inexperienced Iraqi judiciary'. Though they are quite happy to expound at length about the 'rich heritage' of this 'fine people', on this single issue, so it seems, this 'fine [conservative] heritage' is simply not to their taste when it comes to embracing the principle behind the Sixth Commandment. It has, though, been impossible for liberals to disguise the fact that their chief interest lies, not in the pursuit of justice or concerns for the future safety of the Iraqi people, but rather in a Gollum-like pursuit of their own 'precious' liberal agenda.

Whatever the views of the ineffectual United Nations or

rabid *Guardian* or *New York Times* readers, knowledge of Saddam's deeds should lead those who genuinely care for the Iraqi people (if we can gag strident human rights liberals for a moment) to the logical view that perhaps no innocent Iraqi, and a good few others, will be safe while this man lives. Thus if, in the opinion of the lately freed Iraqi people and justice system, the human rights of the Iraqi community outweigh those of the individual's human rights — and particularly *this* individual — who can accuse them of not having a far more morally defensible case than the hand-wringing liberal elites in the West? It is just a shame that so many Western liberals (with the exception of various brave states in the USA) consistently remain more concerned for individual human rights than for communal ones — to the detriment of the spirit of the Sixth Commandment and us all. Of course, it's only my opinion...

The Biblical Case for the Death Penalty
What is not 'only my opinion' is the biblical teaching on the matter. For a start, it is the biblical teaching from which all credible Christians, and nations with a Christian heritage, have taken their lead in respect of any issue — unless of course we happen to be a trendy Archbishop of Canterbury or of the 'church as social club, Bible-nowhere' liberal opinion. And before any liberal or neo-evangelical Christian jumps up demanding the right to their own private interpretation of Scripture, they should know that it is a right specifically denied to them by the author of the Bible himself (Gen. 40:8; 2 Peter 1:20). The fact is that that the consensus mind and teaching of the historic church has always concurred in its interpretation of God's Word in the matter of the state's right to take life, acting as God's agents in doing so.

The ill-informed Christian who believes that faith is a private matter of the heart, should know it is a philosophy neither the Bible nor the historic church teaches. God, through the Bible, teaches 'oneness' of faith which the whole church is to speak — an effective biblical worldview which the church generally, and Christians specifically, are to confess and teach. In an age when the church is progressively abandoning its historic ethos of confessional conformity — and consequently sounding thoroughly incoherent to the world (and to its membership), a mere cacophony of voices — individual Christians are forced, or are only too willing, to offer up their own private, homespun 'take' on contemporary issues. As a consequence (as can be seen from *Why are so many modern Christians so gullible?* in this book), the bulk of modern Christendom no longer possesses a sustainable and coherent pattern of belief or biblical worldview, much less knows what 'the church' believes.

Ours is indeed one of the first generations of the church to perceive the Bible in terms of private interpretation. While the argument in the first half of this essay is set out as a 'matter of opinion' developed from articulated logic, the case being made here is that the genuine Christian — the one who will always humbly bow the knee before God's catholic revelation (the doctrine of *sola Scriptura*, as it is interpreted by the consensus mind of the historic church) — needs to search the pages of Scripture diligently (and listen to the historic church's interpretation of it), allowing the formation of a biblically-informed 'opinion' which includes the use or otherwise of judicial execution.

To anybody who knows their history, including OT and NT history, it will be plainly apparent that the church, both pre- and post- Christ's appearance among us, has consistently held the view that society, though *not* individuals in it, has been granted the divine right to take human life or perform judicial execution. This has especially been granted for the crime of premeditated murder in pursuit of the Sixth Commandment (obedience to God) and its concern to defend the sanctity of human life and thereby the common good (care for one another).

Essentially, this is a simple divine affirmation of the fact that communal rights will always carry more weight than individual rights. As this is an essay on the subject and not an entire book, I will confine my argument here to four critical areas of Scripture which, collectively, contribute to a better Christian understanding and biblical worldview, and arguably the definitive moral case, on the subject. They are:

- The death penalty in the Old Testament context (Exod. 21).
- Christ's teaching in Sermon on the Mount: the general NT context (Matt. 5)
- The divine authority given to all governing authority (Rom.13) *and critically,*
- Jesus before Pilate (John 19).

1. The Death Penalty in the Old Testament context

The Old Testament writings so plainly teach the principle of judicial execution that it needs little comment. Indeed, even those who disagree with its administration today would find themselves hard pressed to argue anything other than the general acceptance of the death penalty for a variety of crimes, including premeditated murder, in the ancient world generally and under the under the Mosaic Law specifically.

Perhaps first, however, we should deal with one old 'chestnut' that still occasionally is raised: that the Sixth Commandment precludes the taking of human life *per se*. It is true that the King James Bible version does translate the passage: 'Thou shalt not kill'. This particular translation has been used by Quakers and pacifists of every Christian and non-Christian hue ever since. But this is simply to rip the passage from its biblical context and to misunderstand the nature and purpose of the Ten Commandments themselves. First and foremost the phrase is perhaps, as in most modern translations, better rendered: 'You shall not murder', restoring completely the missing key element of 'premeditation'. But even if we choose to leave the translation as in the King James Version, then it must be understood that the Ten Commandments represent the totality of the moral Law of God for all humankind and in every generation of humankind. While Jesus repealed and abolished the rites associated with ritual and sacrificial laws, he did not abolish the Law of God (not 'one jot or tittle' of it) but came, as he himself said, to 'fulfil it'. For our purpose here, what we need to grasp is that the Ten Commandments are written specifically as Laws to govern the beliefs and actions of every one of us *as individuals*. Though they are commandments from which communal laws can, and have been, derived, primarily they were/are given to govern individual *moral* behaviour. This is plain enough, in that only an individual, not society, can be guilty of breaking the other Commandments too, such as adultery, bearing false witness, and so on. Thus the Sixth Commandment legislates *against* the individual taking of human life for private or personal motive. But it cannot be extrapolated, however, to place the same injunction on the community, on society. To do so is simply to set the Sixth Commandment adrift from its godly moorings by giving it, alone among the Commandments, a communal connotation (in exactly the same way as Jesus' teachings in the Sermon on the Mount, as we shall see, also have their application) that it cannot bear.

This is very important because it has the consequent effect of separating entirely the individual's responsibilities from that of the community. Thus, though we see that the individual is stripped of the right of premeditated, private retribution and vengeance, we can now see the full force of the Sixth Commandment's thrust in respect of the sanctity of human life, as it is amplified in surrounding passages. The individual may not take human life as an act of private vengeance. But in pursuit of the practical outworking of the Commandment, the community, in the form of the civil authority, can and implicitly — if it is not openly to despise the spirit of the Sixth Commandment — *should* do so. In this the state is merely acting as God's appointed agent to uphold the standard of justice he himself has laid down for all time. In this the state, on behalf of the individual, is upholding the spirit of the Sixth Commandment's moral sanction against the taking of God-given human life (which the murderer has specifically despised and rejected). In this sense, the Commandment itself sees the social rejection of the use of the death penalty in respect of murder both an abrogation of the Law of God and its *own* rejection of the principle of upholding the sanctity of human life in practice.

There is, of course, as the OT itself elsewhere makes clear, a world of difference between premeditated killing for personal gain or private motive, and accidental unpremeditated killing (manslaughter), or killing in war, or even a crime of passion. There is also a vast difference between killing on behalf of, or for the good of, the whole community or nation and premeditated killing for personal reasons. However the Sixth Commandment is rendered, the Bible sets out fully all the various distinctions and the due penalties for causing the death of another human being. One passage which elaborates on the Sixth Commandment and the need for the adoption of the death penalty in society is Exodus 21, which says,

> He who strikes a man so that he dies shall surely be put to death. But if he did not lie in wait, but God delivered him into his hand, then I will appoint for you a place where he may flee. But if a man acts with premeditation against his neighbour, to kill him with guile, you shall take him from my altar, that he may die.

By removing some killing from the private to the public realm in this way, 'vengeance' does indeed 'belong to the Lord'.

Of course, while many Christians would accept that this is the OT position, the modern Christian often tends to the view that the whole moral Law of God (as well as the ritual law of the Jewish nation) was *also* 'set aside' by Christ (i.e. antinomianism: anti-law) when he abolished the other aspects of sacrificial laws and rites. Having asserted that the OT principle is plainly 'pro-death penalty', let us now briefly assess the position post-Sermon on the Mount.

2. *The Sermon on the Mount (Matthew chapters 5-7)*

Because God forgives our sins (when the wages of *all* sin is death), he expects us to reveal that same character of forgiveness and mercy in our own personal lives and dealings, a level of mercy even higher than that practised by our OT believing counterparts (who did not know Christ in Person and consequently could know less than we can concerning the character of God). It was in the Sermon on the Mount that Jesus most clearly articulated this greater degree of personal forgiveness and mercy. He spoke of how each one of us is to approach issues including murder, adultery, oath-making, love, prayer and judging generally, among others. But again the context in which he is speaking is the private realm of individual, personal morality. Alerting us to our very human capacity to judge others, using scales of justice different from those which we would perhaps adopt towards ourselves, he warns us, as of first priority, to 'remove the moat from our own eye'. What a more careful study of this whole passage reveals is Jesus' overriding concern for the area of *personal* ethics, and not the quite separate area of communal or *social* ethics (though the former would undoubtedly affect the latter).

We only have to mention one or two instances to see that

this is logically so. When Jesus raises the issue of 'retaliation' when 'wronged', he is concerned that each of us learns the higher principle of 'turning the other cheek' to the other person (Matt. 5:39). And where someone has stolen our tunic or clothing, we are told to ' let him have your cloak also' (Matt. 5:40). But what if the 'other person' should beat you senseless? Or rob you of everything you own? Are you called simply to become a physical 'doormat' and 'turn the other cheek' to the extent that you 'give him the keys to your house and car', putting you and your family on the street? I do not think so. Clearly, this would make a nonsense of all Godly social order, and anarchy would soon follow. *This* is why God-given authority has been put in place, to act on our behalf to remove the business of upholding authority and the rule of the civil law, for the good of all, from the private and personal realm to that of the social and communal. For justice to be holy, it must be administered within the context of the personal realm — where moral restraint and judgment is to be exercised, as God has exercised it daily for us in being slow to anger and quick to forgive us — and more broadly by society, on our behalf, removing the associated sense of personal grievance and vengeance which can so dominate privatized response.

The fact is that the Sermon on the Mount is primarily concerned with individual Christian ethics, not social ones. This is plain from the context of the whole address as well as from its constituent parts. What the Sermon on the Mount does teach, among much else, is how the twin themes of forgiveness and mercy should become integrated aspects of our personal character and experience: noting that, as God has been slow to judge (condemn) us, so we should be slow to judge (condemn) others. But this does not mean that God does not ultimately judge, nor allow us to judge either. Indeed, not only does God judge or discern, but he also has Paul asking rhetorically, 'Does not the spiritual man judge all things? (1 Cor. 2:15).

One of the major teachings most Christians would do well to recover from the Sermon is the fact that Jesus delivered this prelude to his teachings:

> Do not think that I came to destroy the Law or the Prophets. I did not come to destroy but to fulfil. For assuredly I say to you, till heaven and earth pass away, one jot or one tittle will by no means pass from the law till all is fulfilled. Whoever breaks one of these commandments and teaches men so, shall be called least in the kingdom of heaven; but whoever does and teaches them, he shall be called great in the kingdom of heaven. (Matt. 5:17-19)

Far from removing the social injunction to obey the moral Law of God in the Ten Commandments, and all that flows from them, Christ himself reaffirms this divine instruction. Neither in his teachings in the Sermon on the Mount, nor anywhere else, does Jesus deny or seek to affect society's attitude towards upholding the sanctity of life and, thereby, the right to enforce the death penalty in the case of premeditated murder. It is clear from other areas of the NT that Christ does introduce a powerful element of forgiveness in respect of sins committed, where previously the death penalty had been authorized. In fact, it could be argued that he did so in just about every area *except* that of premeditated murder. As regards this single area, we must look further at the powers of God-ordained civil authority *and*, above all, to Jesus' specific attitude to Pilate's claimed right of life and death over him.

3. Romans 13: The Power of the Governing Authorities

The plainest NT teaching on the nature of the powers of the governing authority, which God gives to man, can be found in Romans chapter 13. Here the distinction between the responsibilities of the governing bodies and the individual are laid bare. Where Jesus taught the individual to 'turn the other cheek', even allowing the theft of not only one tunic but two, society is set an altogether different task. Indeed the whole tone of Paul's teaching concerning the responsibilities of the public authorities is much tougher, as it is made abundantly clear that the individual is to fear the governing authorities as a 'terror' to all who do evil (v.3). Such authority, Paul informs us, has been 'appointed by God' himself, and anyone who resists that authority 'resists the ordnance of God' (v.2). In other words, disobeying governing powers is tantamount to disobeying 'God's minister to you for good'. And, if we 'do evil', then we are to be afraid of those who bear this God-given responsibility, 'for he does not bear the sword in vain; for he is God's minister, an avenger to execute wrath on him who practises evil.'(v.4) We are to be in no doubt that the civil authorities, unlike us as individuals, bear God's own authority when it comes to delivering (no doubt imperfectly) human justice.

We should note that the image of retribution relied upon here is that which affords final, not just temporary, justice, the sword. The sword is, of course, potentially an instrument of death and not of mere chastisement. It could have been described as a 'whip of cords' (which Jesus used to cleanse the Temple) or some other 'gentler' implement. But the *retributive* sword, and none of these others, is what the civil powers are mandated to bear and execute God's wrath on evil.

As we reach verse 8 of Romans 13, however, once again the nature of the teaching changes focus and tone and turns to our personal responsibilities to one another. And we find all of the same key elements of forgiveness and mercy to the fore, just as Jesus expounded them in his Sermon on the Mount. What we must understand from all this is that personal and social ethics are not the same thing. And in one instance where the two are in high profile juxtaposition, Jesus' trial before Pilate, the full extent of the powers of the state in respect of life and death issues, for the higher sake of the whole community, comes, as nowhere else, into sharp focus.

4. *Jesus before Pilate*

Without doubt the most telling biblical evidence in respect of Jesus' view on the state's use of the death penalty in the NT era comes from his own trial before the Roman Governor of Judea, Pontius Pilate. Paraded before Pilate, the Jewish leadership were vociferous in their accusations against Jesus; charges which, under OT Jewish Law, carried the sanction of 'ultimate justice'. But only the occupying power, and thus the Roman governor himself, was mandated to perform the act of judicial killing in Israel at that time. Being aware that he was being coerced by the Jewish leaders into finding guilty a man in whom he personally saw little or no guilt, and taken aback by Jesus' apparent unwillingness to defend himself, Pilate asks Christ whether has understood that he, Pilate, has the power/authority to crucify (kill) him or to release him (John 10). Given that this exchange, on the key issue of the nature of the power invested in the state, would henceforth resonate around the world for millennia to come, here, *par excellence,* is the platform from which Jesus could denounce all human right to take not only *his* life, but *any* human life, henceforth. *But he did not take it.*

What we find instead is something radically different. Jesus' concern was not for his own life, nor was it even to *deny* Pilate's claim to wielding the power of life and death over him. Instead Jesus chose to make two very different, highly instructive points, answering Pilate thus:

> You could have no power at all against me unless it

had been given you from above. Therefore the one who delivered me to you has the greater sin. (John 19:11)

First, Jesus was perfectly content to cede to Pilate (as the due civil authority) the right of jurisdiction over his life. But where Pilate's plain opinion was his by 'Roman might', Jesus sought to disabuse him by locating that *right* in a different and higher authority than Rome. Second, he also made clear that the Jewish leaders, his accusers, were more responsible than the Roman authorities for his crucifixion. Thus Jesus duly affirmed Pilate's notion of *rightful* civil authority in matters of judicial execution, while taking pains to identify where, primarily, responsibility for delivering him wrongfully to that authority — and thus taking his life — actually lay. Jesus himself nowhere in Scripture denies, negates or amends the power of the governing authorities to administer justice, tempered in some areas and on some occasions with mercy, as they see fit. Indeed Jesus recognized only too well that in exerting this power, in his case over life and death, Pilate was merely acting as God's agent. It was this that Christ wanted Pilate — *and, through the Scriptures, the world* — to know, as of greatest importance at this most critical moment in all of human history.

Not a hint anywhere here, when the matter could easily have been laid to rest for all time, that the use of the death penalty was an immoral, unchristian or, somehow, ungodly or unsanctified act, in God's greater scheme of things.

We should note that those who oppose the death penalty do not simply say that the death penalty is wrong: rather they say that the death penalty is wrong *because of the danger of killing an innocent person*. The same thing was true for Jesus, however, and could have been put forward as an argument in any age. Clearly it is not an argument that carries great weight in divine 'circles'. All liberal thinking,

Christian and non-Christian, regarding the death penalty, lacks the force of persuasive argument in terms of logic or biblical teaching. Instead it tends to be reduced to arguing *against* it in terms of mostly hypothetical, extreme, or worst-case scenarios to frighten us into banning it altogether. But if we operated on this principle in any other area of the law, the whole rule of law would simply collapse.

Liberals say, 'ah, but the death penalty is different. Any mistake here cannot be rectified!' But even if this fear may be true in an occasional instance, it simply lacks integrity to extend the argument to most or every case. What of those individuals who are not only mass murderers, but who were caught on camera plainly committing the act? Those who openly admit their crimes and who claim they will kill again? Those for whom, through their vast financial resources, languishing in a prison cell will be no bar at all to authorizing yet more murders? And what of the large number of individuals who are freed and who *do* murder again? How, in such *plain* cases, does liberal reasoning make *any* sense at all? What liberal thinking does successfully is to neutralize the effect of the law at the very point that its concern to uphold the sanctity of life is most revealed, and is thus most threatening to the common good.

What is made clear from a thorough familiarity with the Scriptures on all of these points is that God, in the OT, made the death penalty a legal fixture in respect of murder and many other offences. What is clear from the New Testament is that Jesus sets a number of specific precedents which go a long way to assuaging the number of crimes for which the death penalty might in future be ordained, but that this does not include premeditated murder. An examples of those offences for which the death penalty is no longer applicable would be adultery — it was Jesus himself who forgave the woman caught in adultery, making clear her sin but telling her to 'sin no more' (John 8:1-11). But this in no way introduces that same degree of divine leniency and social clemency into the area of the most heinous of crimes, premeditated murder. Indeed, Jesus' responses to Pilate at his own trial, dictate that the very opposite is true.

A personal anecdote

I am reluctant to play the liberal's game and rely on support from personal anecdotes. Even so, I will include one as a practical illustrative purpose. Many years ago I was a senior officer in charge of processing legal work for the Crown Court section of the national Crown (now Public) Prosecution Service in the north London area. One morning I happened to be in the Magistrates Court section office and glanced through upcoming cases. These were papers relating to crimes perpetrated over the previous twenty-four hours, which were for use at initial hearings that morning. One file in particular caught my eye. It bore an unusual and very familiar name. It was the same name as the father of a teenage girl who was a member of my own church house group. Her father was also a member of our church. Upon closer inspection, the victim of a killing the afternoon before did indeed turn out to be this young girl's father, my fellow worshipper. It transpired that in the course of managing his hotel business he had confronted a man who was threatening hotel guests with a knife. Without any provocation, the man stabbed this fine Christian man, killing him.

Shocked by coming across this case file, I turned to the killer's previous convictions to find that this same man had committed an almost identical crime some eight years before (and had attempted to do so on other occasions). Because the civil authorities had failed to fulfil their duty on the earlier occasion and take this man's life (or at least incarcerate him for life, which is the due penalty for murder), innocent blood had again been shed, and the community had, once again, not been protected as it should have been. The liberal will come up with all sorts of excuses for this. But the simple fact is that a justice system, which sought rather to 'rehabilitate' a premeditating (plain from the number of occasions he attempted this crime) murderer had failed in its abiding duty to protect innocent blood. The judicial execution of this man would, humanly speaking, have saved the life of my Christian friend and, just as significantly, saved his family and friends from lifelong pain and suffering over their grievous loss. But, to add insult to injury, they know that not only should this man have not been walking the streets at all, but that he probably is today doing so again — and in flagrant violation of God's ordnances.

Whilst I am a supporter of the death penalty for premeditated murder, I do not say that it need be invoked for all murders. A crime of passion, for instance, is a clear area where clemency may justly affect the severity of the sentence. I am thinking of the more obvious premeditated murders, those where mercy must, by plain definition, run out. Mass murderers and child killers, to mention but two, would come under this heading. But the liberal might ask: could you be the one to 'press the button' and 'cold-bloodedly' take another's life? This is another liberal irrelevance, because the simple answer should, for the Christian at least, always be 'yes' — and for this reason. God has specifically denied me, as an individual, the right to take life, but, if I am acting as a dispassionate agent of the civil magistrate, it is my very duty. Acting as an agent of the state, as the God-ordained human authority, is to act without malice at all, merely to fulfil God's instruction. Thus proper and appropriate judicial killing is not to *play* God, but to act *for* God.

As we have seen, the liberal argument that capital punishment is *de facto* wrong, illogical and intellectually stunted. Neither is it, perversely, the prevailing view among broader populations. When the Oklahoma City bomber Timothy McVeigh made his court appearance, having confessed to blowing up and murdering over 140 people, 8 out of 10 Americans believed that he should pay with his life. This, as a Gallup Poll pointed out, included as many as 20 per cent who normally were against the death penalty.[5]

I for one am bemused by the inverted logic of the liberal who points to the 'sanctity of human life' as being the reason for *not* sending some murderers to their deaths. For a start, if we are talking about humanists and atheists, what on earth do they mean by 'sanctity of life'? Sanctity, by definition, mean 'holy' or 'sacred'. To whom is it 'holy' or 'sacred'? To them? To use the word 'sanctity' is fine if one points to a higher authority. But on whom, except themselves, with their illogical arguments, can the liberal humanist call? Neither should we allow them to bluster endlessly about 'worst case scenario' examples to obscure the need to uphold the law and the sanctity of life, as it is meant to be upheld. We all know that not every conviction is dubious or spurious, but that most are 100 per cent correct. Indeed, some criminals have no qualms about understanding that their own crimes ought to deliver them to 'ultimate justice' as the 'proper' punishment, and they are upset when capital punishment is denied them!

Conclusion

The Christian, in particular, should therefore realize that it is an entirely justifiable belief, logically reasoned and biblically reasoned, to hold that the state *is* empowered to adopt and carry out the death penalty as a moral imperative in respect of convicted murderers. Further, the logic of those who argue against the death penalty *per se* will *always* be questionable. They themselves need to be clear whether their objection is based upon the 'in case we make a mistake' argument (as there will always be very clear instances, such as with Saddam Hussein, when *no* mistake is possible); or the 'sanctity of human life' principle (when they will not be able, as human secularists, to justify their right to adopt the word 'sanctity' when they, unlike Christians, Jews and Moslems and others, have no 'gold standard' of morality to which they may appeal). Or whether, as is perhaps far nearer the mark, they are simply sensitive, liberal souls who wish to impose their irrational and ill-thought-out, yet highly vocal and dangerous, views upon us all.

The reality, as with most liberals, is that they will angrily 'dodge' from argument to argument in order to boost an intellectually compromised and threadbare case; not having any real notion where the crux of their true objection lies, because they have simply never really thought through the logic of their position. As a practising Christian who is constantly amazed at the wisdom of God and the futile human philosophies of men, for my own part I can only concur with George W. Bush when, based on the evidence in the public arena, he concludes that Saddam Hussein should face 'ultimate justice'. But that is a matter for the Iraqi judiciary, as indeed it should be.

---

1 Neil Postman, *Amusing Ourselves To Death: Public Discourse in the Age of Show Business* (London: Methuen, 1986).

2 Leaving aside the *individual* human rights of the unborn child, how long will we allow liberals to maintain the fictitious 'opinion' that abortion does not involve other members of the community (doctors, nurses etc.) in the moral dilemma, as well as the rest of the community (you and me) in the associated fiscal costs?

3 When Christ addressed the issue of the taking of human life in the Sermon on the Mount, the whole thrust of that sermon was one of *personal* (individual), not *social* (communal), ethics. He was telling his hearers not what rights and responsibilities society had, but what rights and responsibilities they each had. Think about it. You and I can act in a restrained manner and 'turn the other cheek'. But how could a court of law, acting on behalf of the community, do so? Also, when Jesus stood

before Pilate he nowhere denies Pilate's right to take life: instead he draw Pilate's attention to where his authority to do so came from.

[4] In the West, public opinion consistently polls in favour of the reintroduction of the death penalty for premeditated murder, with 54 per cent in favour in the UK and only 36 per cent against (ICM Poll conducted on behalf of the *Sunday Telegraph*, Nov. 2003); and with a massive 74 per cent in favour in the USA (Gallup Poll, 19 May, 2003).

[5] Jeffrey M. Jones, 'The Death Penalty' special report (Gallup Poll, August 2002).

ISSUES: self-defence & weapons
of mass destruction

2
WAR & PEACE - Part 1
The Pre-Emptive Strike: is it moral?

*When you see a rattlesnake poised to strike,
you do not wait until he has struck before you crush him*[1]
Franklin D. Roosevelt

There's been much hand-wringing in the West over the morality of pre-emptive strikes of force by national governments, especially in the wake of the new global war, the War on Terror.[2] For many, the invasive rooting out of terrorists in the cities and caves of Afghanistan by the USA post-9/11 was somewhat understandable, for some just about acceptable. For others, invasion and regime change in Iraq was the unacceptable face of imperial interventionism. The issue of justifiable moral response is perhaps clearer when self-defence and retribution are the clear reaction to overt aggressive acts (the USA declaring war after the infamous attack on Pearl Harbour), but less so when self-defence is mooted as the reason for pre-emptive strike action (the Israeli destruction of the Iraqi nuclear facility in the 1980s). The 2003 invasion of Iraq in some ways clouded the distinction between these two areas. On the one hand, in the wake of 9/11, there were alleged links between al-Qu'eda and Saddam's regime, which represented a potential direct threat to the security of many nations[3] and — after twelve years of blatant defiance of the world community — the need finally to enforce UN resolutions which marked the disengagement at the end of the 1991 war.

I do not here propose to discuss the morality of the invasion of Iraq. I will leave that discussion to part 2 of this essay. But if the media and public fall-out after the invasion of Iraq did anything, it focused our minds on the whole issue of the morality of the pre-emptive strike and foreign 'interventionism'. If the world has struggled with these issues, in my experience it is fair to observe that most modern Christians have *not*, with the simplistic 'all-war-is-evil' approach of the vocal, liberal church leadership gaining notoriety and apparently speaking for many. In particular, it is the notion of the invasion of sovereign territory (national states being set in place by God himself) that seems to exercise many. It is right, however, that we do not merely follow the herd in this, and especially the liberal-dominated academy and church hierarchy, but rather develop our position from a Bible-centred worldview. Before we get under way though, we shall need to establish one or two key ground rules to clear our path ahead.

For the purposes of this article I will assume (and not argue — that would take a book in its own right) two elements which the world commonly accepts and which the Bible and the historic church have long taught. First, that Christians are not, except under appropriate circumstances, called to practise pacifism. When all is said and done, Christ was no practising pacifist when he took time out to make a knotted cord (a weapon) to violently assault the cynical moneychangers and overturn their tables in the Temple courtyard. This was no mere outburst of spontaneous anger, but rather a calculated and premeditated act, having checked out the Temple courtyard activity the night before (see Mark 11:11).

It was an action fuelled by righteous indignation at the terrible rip-offs which were taking place on sanctified ground and in the name of God. Later that week, however, he would partake of an entirely pacifist action when he went 'as a lamb to the slaughter' on Good Friday. Generally speaking, instances of passive inactivity are not to be the norm for man, especially when the more appropriate need is an angry outburst against spiritual and moral hypocrisy.

Contrary to widely held humanistic opinion and the populist church worldview, man is not 'basically good', but, in God's terms, is sinful by nature (Rom. 3:23). Jesus and the Bible make it perfectly clear that the devil is at large in the world and that he is our evil adversary (1 Peter 5:8), doing all he can to stoke the fires of man's sinfulness. But man is not called to flee from him and his evil (unless in the form of temptation): rather he is called proactively to resist him (1 Peter 5:9) and expose his 'works of darkness' (Eph.5:11). This is not passive activity, but a highly proactive one. Second, I shall assume, for the sake of this article, that we have landed on Planet Reality and that we all (which some won't of course) hold the 'just war' position. War is indeed 'hell', with a tendency to cause indiscriminate suffering and pain by its nature, but God has used it often enough for *his* own purposes by raising up one nation to punish another (2 Kings 17:21-23; Jer.34:21). And nothing Jesus said in his famous Sermon on the Mount, which essentially addresses *personal* moral responsibilities and ethics and not *communal* and *national* ones, changes the fact that there will always be 'wars and rumours of wars' (Matt. 24:6).

War is an inescapable fact of human existence and will be until, as Christians believe, Christ returns. So let us be realists, and not sentimentalists who believe, against all the evidence, that man is somehow going to eradicate war. If, as Christ teaches, man is sinful and 'not good', then how is man to achieve anything remotely approaching a peaceful human Utopia on this earth? History alone suggests a very different future. In doing so, we shall leave behind the arguments of theoretic pipe-smoking, corduroy-trousered academics, anti-war urban terrorists, retro-hippies, Anglican Archbishops, the bulk of the modern liberal church clergy and academy and all Planet Unreality pacifists, including, of course, French politicians and the United Nations. Chillingly, the words adorning a wall in the modern UN HQ building, 'Peace and Safety', are the very words the apostle Paul adopts saying 'When they say "Peace and Safety!" then sudden destruction comes upon them' (1 Thess. 5:3).

Having cleared the decks of the 'other-worldly' spiritual New Agers in our midst, the rest of us can acknowledge that war, dreadful and hateful as it may be, is not only morally justifiable before God, but may from time to time be the only moral course to take. However, though we may perhaps feel ourselves comfortable with pre-emptive action during 'wartimes', we may find the issue far less clear in what we perceive and know as 'times of peace'. It is this area to which we now turn.

The morality of self-defence

'Turning the other cheek' in the face of some intemperate provocation is certainly the plain teaching of the Christian church. But, as I have written elsewhere, when Jesus gave this and many other teachings during his Sermon on the Mount, it was in the context of minor and provocative violence and personal vengeance. Where the issue of more serious sustained and dangerous violence has occurred, the matter of vengeance (vengeance 'being mine' says the Lord) is removed from the personal realm altogether and given into the public realm, as a matter for communal judgment and response. But in the case of nation states, it is plain enough that God has often taken his vengeance by raising up one nation to punish another nation.

Thus when the gangster Nazi regime in Berlin decided to obliterate the London skyline in 1940, we may not extrapolate from this that what Christ would have wanted was a mass 'cheek-turning' in the streets during the next wave of attacks. To allow the Luftwaffe to do their worst, was tantamount to inviting yet more unjust violence by providing them with a green light to continue — and to rearrange large tracts of Manchester, too.

Historically, the right to self-defence, both personal and national, has always been a well-understood principle by most, including the Christian church. If we hold to the notion of the sanctity of human life as being in any way meaningful, then it must therefore be our right to defend ourselves and others, employing what the law determines is 'appropriate' or 'proportionate' force to that end. In this way then, we must admit that there has to be a limit to Christ's injunction to the individual to 'turn the other cheek', especially where doing so could lead to serious injury or death. Indeed the very example of turning the cheek which Christ uses, implicitly envisages no harmful threat coming to the body or person (in the form of bruising or serious bodily harm), but a mild chastisement or a humiliating effrontery (a slap or such). Anything beyond that must therefore bring (if we accept the hermeneutical principle that Scripture interprets Scripture) other biblical principles into play.

For a start, assuming that a pacifist response may in *some* circumstances be appropriate, even in the face of the severest violence, is surely the exception rather than the norm (Jesus' 'torture' was part of God's plan). Pacifism, or turning the other cheek, is largely for the realm of individual response where imminent serious danger is not present.

Jesus' example of the 'slapped cheek' suggests that it is also largely in situations where the principle of 'swallowing one's pride' arises. In other situations it is plainly not taught as a life principle. Whilst there are many who like to think of themselves as pacifists, I have long maintained that most are more 'theoretic pacifists' than they believe. When it comes down to 'brass tacks', given the right circumstances and provocation, I would contend that most people would relinquish their pacifism in an instant.

The *High Noon* Syndrome
Take the situation where a loved one, perhaps a small child, is being threatened with a gun. Being some distance away, the only way you know you can prevent the aggressor from pulling the trigger is by using the gun in your own hand. The bottom line is: do you pull the trigger or do you stand by and watch your innocent young child die at the hands of an evil killer? Do you see what I mean? There are lots of *theoretical* pacifists, but few who would remain so in the most trying of circumstances. Just like Grace Kelly's Quaker character in *High Noon*, very few of us could allow evil to succeed in taking away our nearest and dearest while we stood idly by. As Edmund Burke said, 'Evil flourishes while good men stand idly by'.

I have a distinct recollection of wrestling, as a new Christian, with the morality highlighted in *High Noon*. It was one of my favourite films. Before becoming a Christian I had no cause to question Marshall Will Kane (Gary Cooper)'s actions. It just *seemed* the right thing to do. But knowing the views of some older Christians who tended toward pacifist views, I had to rethink the whole thing. Was Kane right to stay and fight, after all? Should he have left town and avoided the undoubted bloodshed that staying would mean? By facing the evil, was he not bringing it upon the whole township (as many of the townsfolk, including his new Quaker wife, claimed)? Was Kane guilty of immorally *pre-empting* trouble and ushering in unnecessary violence? To agree with what the sheriff did in the film would, inescapably, mean agreeing that using guns, enjoining violence and killing, really is morally justifiable. It was all a little too much for a young Christian with little clear teaching and it took me some time to work it all out. But what it boiled down to was this: that the issue in *High Noon* was not violence *for the sake of violence:* rather was it largely unavoidable and inevitable. At the very best it was violence that could only have been deferred for a short time, since Miller's band were bent on murderous intent and exacting vengeance on the man who had put away their leader. As Kane explained, had they run (as they began to do) they would almost certainly have been caught out in the open, in an even more defenceless position. Such was the hatred of Frank Miller that he would have pursued them wherever they went. Far better then to stay put, ready to defend yourself and your family in an advantageous position. In short, Kane did what was right. But so, too, did his Quaker wife (Grace Kelly) when she shot and killed one of the would-be killers in defence of her husband — and in the process denied the validity of her own theoretic moral pacifism *in the face of rank evil.*

In defending himself, Kane did indeed pre-empt the violence. While the Bible teaches man to 'flee temptation', it does not teach him to 'flee evil'. Rather man is called to expose and resist evil, as we have seen. So how do these moral realities play out in the arena of world affairs?

An example from recent history
When Adolf Hitler annexed the Sudetenland and made it part of Germany, the whole world, including the USA and Britain, turned a blind eye, leaving an invaded people to their fate. Now emboldened, and believing no Western power

would react, Hitler next invaded Poland. In 1939 Britain's Neville Chamberlain flew to Berlin and returned brandishing a piece of paper signed by Adolf Hitler, hailing his visit as a coup which had brought 'peace in our time'. We call this acceptance of evil gain, in an attempt to avert further evil, 'appeasement'. The history of appeasement, as one finds time and again by leafing through the history books, has a very long and distinctly undistinguished record. Just like the bullies who made our life misery in the schoolyard, it was not until someone stood up to the aggressor that we found two things: resisting evil does work, and that bullies, more often than not, turn out to be cowards at heart. In 1939 Great Britain finally listened to the prophetic warnings of Winston Churchill. It awoke to the truth that if it did not honour its pledge to defend the sovereignty of European allies, other countries and Britain itself could well be next.

Though Britain did declare war against Germany, for the sake of others as well as for itself, it was in truth acting in self-defence and pre-emptively. No one seriously thinks that Britain's action then was anything other than right and moral, indeed the noble thing to do. If anyone still harbours doubt that the Bible teaches pacifism, they should look to the example of Jesus Christ himself.

Christ cleansing the Temple

When Jesus entered Jerusalem at the beginning of the Jewish Passover, during that first Easter week, he made his way, not to the public market square, but to the precincts of the Temple. Anyone not understanding why, should appreciate that it is a recurring theme of Scripture that God's judgment always comes first to his own, the household of God — the church. It was already late evening and, having taken a good look around at the activities taking place there, Jesus left. The following day however, the first thing he did was to return. And there he did something entirely unexpected which undoubtedly fast-tracked him on the road to Calvary. What happened that morning was the overturning of the tables of the moneychangers. This was Jesus entering 'his Father's house' and specifically confronting the evil which was flourishing there in full public view. Of all places where evil should *not* be stomached, the Jewish moneychangers were systematically fleecing pilgrims from near and far, particularly the Gentile worshippers. And they were doing it at the heart of the worshipping community and with the full connivance of the Temple authorities. It is notable that Jesus did not take time to present a petition and argue his case. But neither was this a spontaneous outburst of uncontrolled anger.

He did not simply go around pleading with these merchants to act more righteously. Their crime was beyond argument. What he planned was entirely violent, *pre-emptive* action. He even took time out to make a weapon, a cord of knots, to reveal the measure of God's wrath they had brought upon themselves. No wonder the Temple authorities saw Jesus as a threat. He was a threat not only to their authority and power, but also to their income. Here then is the Son of God himself setting forth a righteous example of one prepared to go to great lengths to cleanse the house of God in a pre-emptive defence of God's name and honour, as well as for the greater good of the people.

So we have seen that when it comes to world events, to doing what is the Godly, moral thing, and acting in self-defence against impending violence, the principle of pre-emption is made out. But how does this principle apply to us with regard to the events of our time?

The Problem of Weapons of Mass Destruction

All that we have said so far is perhaps less than controversial for most who know their Bible teaching — indeed most who take a common sense and objective perspective on these things. When cynical dictators build up massed armies on our border, it is almost certainly not a unilateral act of détente that they have in mind! Responding to such a build-up by moving our own army into a defensive position may exacerbate the problem, but it is only what any self-respecting nation must do in defence of its citizens. But what if you knew the build-up to be a prelude to full invasion, as with Hitler's blitzkrieg across Europe? Is it not morally defensible, if a nation has the strength, to pre-empt the invasion and disable the aggressive forces before they can perform their evil? Some would say that *not* to do so — and I would be one of them — may well amount to an act of national treachery which would probably lead to even more death and destruction than might otherwise have been the case. Had the world reacted to stop Hitler earlier, who knows how much death and destruction may have been averted — not least the Jewish holocaust of six million deaths. Pre-empting the actions of others is something of an inexact, subjective 'science'. But in the age of the indiscriminate mayhem that can be caused by weapons of mass destruction (WMD), which is undoubtedly the greatest specific threat to mankind today, pre-emption can become even more complicated.

When the Americans dropped the hydrogen bombs on Hiroshima and Nagasaki, it was the final act of a war in which the USA was not the aggressor. It had also become clear that the Japanese, because of their particular code of honour, were intent on fighting to the last. In other words, a lot more Americans and allies would have to die fighting to put an end to Japan's aggression. The stark calculation was that this was one way of shortening the war and at least saving the lives of thousands of Americans who would otherwise die because of the evil of those in the Japanese leadership. While the bombs took many lives, it undoubtedly saved many others. In short, it was a decision taken as the 'lesser of two evils'.

But what of Israel's bombing of Iraqi factories which

intelligence information alleged were close to developing nuclear weaponry — when Iraq's stated goal was the destruction of Israel. Iraq under Saddam Hussein had, as other Arab national leaders, long called for the annihilation of the State of Israel and had continually demonstrated its evil intent towards that sovereign state. In this regard I would argue that morally there is little or no difference at all between pre-empting an attack and adopting a 'first-strike' policy to deal with impending evil, whether it be massed armies on our borders or a nuclear attack from a neighbour bent on delivering weapons of mass destruction into our backyard.

The only difference will be convincing the court of international law as well as the court of international opinion, that your intelligence was accurate and that you were therefore morally justified in taking pre-emptive action in your own self-defence. All of which brings us neatly around to why Saddam Hussein was removed from power as a result of the invasion of Iraq in 2003.

---

[1] Franklin D Roosevelt, speaking of the threat of Nazism, FDR Fireside Chat to the Nation, 11 September, 1941. See www.usmm.org/fdr/rattlesnake.html.

[2] I am fully aware that some leading liberal print columnists entirely refute the notion that there is in fact a War on Terror. These include Simon Jenkins and Stephen Glover (no relation!) and various others who write for leading newspapers and *The Spectator* magazine. It seems that these men are in a state of denial, given that terrorists declared war, not the West.

[3] It is abundantly clear that there were extensive links between Saddam's regime and the al-Qu'eda leadership as Stephen F. Hayes important new book *The Connection: How Al Qaeda's Collaboration with Saddam Hussein Has Endangered America* makes abundantly clear.

ISSUES: The anatomy & morality of
the war in Iraq

3
WAR & PEACE - Part II
The Invasion of Iraq: was it justified?

One year on from the US-led invasion of Iraq in 2003 and the resumption — yes, resumption — of the 1991 war, the public debate concerning the moral justification for the invasion rumbles on. In the West, the chief debate has revolved almost exclusively around the issue of the failure to find stockpiles of WMD.

In the light of the many post-war problems experienced by the occupying US-led coalition, the anti-war lobby has turned up the political heat on the US President and the UK Prime Minister, especially over their pre-war assurance that Saddam both possessed WMD and was intent on using them. But when the reasons for invasion and the removal of Saddam from power are reviewed away from the rhetoric of the anti-war lobby, and the somewhat vacillating convictions of the modern armchair critic, we might wonder just what all the fuss is about. While I, as a former press advisor to, and spokesman for, one of the highest-ranking public officials in the UK,[1] have been mystified by Tony Blair's public mishandling of the WMD issue,[2] it seems to me that the hand-wringing over WMD by the West's intelligentsia is a classic example of taking one's political eye 'off the ball'.

Saddam is a man who is a serial invader of sovereign nations (Iran and Kuwait) and has dropped bombs on a third (Israel), a nation he has continually threatened to exterminate by using WMD. And, as we noted in part 1 of this essay, his links with al Qu'eda and their declared war on America and the West have been well established. The only remaining area of disagreement was whether 'co-operation' had gone beyond the 'planning' stage and reached operational levels. Even so, what is known fact is that Saddam has the blood of hundreds of thousands of people on his hands (some literally by his own hand), that he is responsible for the displacement of a further two million of his own countrymen, and that he had used WMD in his war with Iran and against his own citizens. And in being responsible for these actions, he has, for twelve years, been in defiance of the terms of the 1991 ceasefire, by which the world community via the United Nations required him to disarm — with seventeen UN resolutions in pursuit of the same goal up to 2003.

Amazingly, however, the real scandal is why, for a full twelve years, the UN did not possess the will to enforce their own resolutions aimed at disarming Saddam — the only reason why he remained in power after his defeat in 1991. Eventually, the patience of the USA (whose citizens had given their lives to defeat Saddam in 1991), and the patience of other members of the world community, finally snapped and, in the face of mounting evidence of Saddam's relentless and evil intentions, the UN's moral duty was done for them.

The West's hand-wringing over WMD

The hand-wringing of the West's elite almost beggars belief when it comes to whether or not Saddam possessed WMD after the 2003 invasion. We *know* that Saddam possessed

WMD because he used them in his war against Iran in the 1980s and against his own people, even destroying a whole Kurdish village in the 1990s. So we *know* he had no compunction in using them on both domestic and foreign soil. We know also that Saddam pursued a relentless course aimed at developing biological, chemical and missile weaponry, even after his defeat during the 'first' Gulf War in 1991. After countless denials to the UN, Saddam eventually admitted that chemical programmes did in fact exist, but that they were for purely 'domestic use'. We know better. What we learn from his actions right up to the invasion are two keys things: that Saddam was bent on developing and using WMD and that he would do *anything* to hide this fact from international prying eyes.

All of this is today a matter of public record with the UN itself. At the cessation of hostilities in 1991, having removed the Iraqi army from sovereign Kuwaiti soil, the UN-sanctioned allied army made a tactical mistake. It left Saddam Hussein in power, fearing the backlash from other Arab nations if an invasion of Iraq was undertaken. Instead, on 3 April 1991 the UN passed Security Council resolution 687 requiring 'that Iraq unconditionally accept, under international supervision, the destruction, removal or rendering harmless of its weapons of mass destruction, ballistic missiles with a range over 150 kilometres, and related production facilities and equipment'. The resolution also made a requirement of 'Iraq's full compliance with the ban on these weapons and missiles'. On 6 April 1991 Iraq agreed to accept resolution 687.

But what followed was yet another shameful twelve years of Saddam defying the will of the world community through countless UN resolutions and pursuing a covert programme of continuing to develop his WMD capability. To list just a few examples of Saddam's disregard for the terms of his 'surrender' on the basis of compliance with UN conditions, we might note from the outset systematic Iraqi non-compliance:

June 1991 — Iraqi personnel fire warning shots to prevent UN inspectors intercepting Iraqi vehicles carrying nuclear-related equipment, and deny access to an inspection site.

September 1991 — When the UN inspectors find large amounts of documentation relating to Iraq's efforts to acquire nuclear weapons, Iraqi officials confiscate some of them. Iraq also blocks the helicopters used by the UN team.

October 1991 — Iraq declares the ongoing monitoring and verification programme as 'unlawful'.

These represent only a tiny proportion of Saddam's infractions over the years, revealing his disdain for international will. You might think that any international organization with integrity would begin to take serious umbrage at such high-handed non-compliance by a defeated aggressor nation. Not the UN, however. Sufficient for the UN over the years was a litany of repeat resolutions all demanding the same thing: compliance to disarm. Thus the tone was set for over a decade, with every year accruing a catalogue of Iraqi procrastination and refusals to comply, with a new resolution and only grudging and partial compliance being the consistent response. UN inspectors were refused access to a host of critical and 'presidential' sites. Stories abounded of Iraq vehicles disappearing out of the back gate of compounds as UN inspectors approached the front gate. In 1992 Iraq was forced to declare the existence of 'previously undeclared ballistic missiles, chemical weapons and associated materials'. Veiled threats were issued against Allied patrol aircraft, which in turn threatened the security of UN inspectors.

By 1994, the defiance of Saddam's government was

such that Iraq began deploying troops toward the Kuwaiti border once more. Not a year passed without serious non-compliance issues being raised. And they were met with yet more UN resolutions and only partial and stuttering Iraqi compliance. Through it all, what remained unchanged was the Iraqi president's determined pursuance of a WMD capability. UN resolutions had also called for 'Full, final and complete disclosure' of Iraq's various biological, chemical and missile programmes. In November 1995 Iraq provided the UN with its *second* 'Full, final and complete disclosure of its prohibited missile programme'. That *same* month the Jordanian Government intercepted a large shipment of high-grade missile components destined for Iraq (indeed some components were actually found inside Iraq). A subsequent investigation discovered that Iraqi authorities and missile facilities had never given up their attempted 'acquisition of sophisticated guidance and control components for proscribed missiles'.

Bizarre as it sounds, during the period up to 1999, the UN was forced to require, and did receive, from the Iraq leader, five (count them, five!) 'Full, final and complete disclosures of its prohibited biological weapons programme'. And it received *three* similar 'Full and final disclosures' for Iraq's prohibited missile programmes. A programme of international sanctions and the UN-instigated 'oil-for-food' project aimed at aiding the Iraqi people were just as cynically abused (as we now know, directly causing the deaths of countless children and vulnerable adults) by the authorities in Iraq.

One might wonder what manner of supervising agency would stomach such a cynical and systematic strategy of defiance and deception, and *for twelve years*! It was, after all, a comprehensive strategy of non-compliance with the UN's own *unconditional* resolution 687 — a *ceasefire only* measure, in 1991. In the wake of a world alerted to the real threat from such weapons by the increasingly proactive network of international terrorism — and Saddam's own known links with those terrorists — it perhaps is unsurprising that parts of the international community might run out of patience. Amazingly, the UN's consistent response was to do nothing meaningful about it. Without doubt, what energized the USA in particular to lose patience with the UN's indolent prevarication, was its recognition of the new world order which it (and indeed all Western society) faced post-9/11. Neither was it lost on Britain that it too would be a prime target for al-Qu'eda and other Islamofascist groups who, like Saddam, also professed a determination to possess and use WMD, if it too did not act.

This is a terrorism that recognizes only too well that it cannot win its battles using conventional forces. It has largely employed guerrilla tactics to date. But the prospect of the acquisition of WMD affords it a whole new strategy. Having demonstrated its capabilities by using planes as WMD against the West, it was plain enough (and the terrorists' stated aim) that the use of biological and chemical WMD were quite legitimate. The West's first target therefore was the sanctuary which Afghanistan had become, as 'home' to countless terrorist camps, but especially the al-Qu'eda network and Osama Bin Laden, who planned the attacks on the World Trade Centre buildings. No one was too surprised, therefore, when the US decided to respond to the murderous attack on its own soil by clearing out that small nest of particularly nasty vipers. But next up would be the 'unfinished business' of Iraq and its president's relentless pursuit of WMD. He had already proved his credentials in using them.

Acknowledging the mistake of not putting an end to Saddam's regime in 1991, the USA, with the UK, pushed for the world community, via the UN, finally to sanction military action against a regime which had defied the world long enough and which had also been shown to be pursuing its own quest for WMD. But, after twelve years of deception, and the undoubted movement of prohibited weapons paraphernalia, the world community remained uncertain as to what the true position over Iraq's WMD capability was. The intelligence agencies, however, were in no doubt (fuelled, as it later transpired, by embellished information from some Iraqi dissidents). Certainly the UN inspectors could not provide a clear picture after years of trying.

Whatever the reasons for the USA and Britain pushing the UN finally to act, they were undoubtedly right to do so, given the troubling international circumstances and Saddam's enduring 'rogue state' status. That the UN was not prepared to act on the failure of Saddam to comply with its seventeen resolutions demanding disarmament in respect of WMD was, and remains, to its shame. That the patience of the USA and the UK had run out and that they, recognizing the genuine threat posed to the world from a man who had already demonstrated his preparedness in using them, is to their great credit. Above all, however, what this ought to focus our minds on is the growing moral bankruptcy of the United Nations, in whom far too many of the world's liberal elites are prepared to invest their hopes for mankind. While the UN may have a place in helping to feed the world's poor, it has increasingly proven itself impotent when it comes to moral action whenever enforcement is required, because of the pure self-interest (as we shall see) of some of the UN's more proactive 'big-hitters'.

The overarching truth here is that what has been termed the 'Second Gulf War' by some, is in fact no more than a resumption of an unfinished war: a war where disengagement was conditional upon the terms of resolution 687, which effected a *conditional* ceasefire. The unequivocal condition laid down was for the *unconditional* 'destruction, removal and rendering harmless' of Iraq's WMD and 'related facilities and equipment'. Because of Saddam's duplicitous activities over twelve years and the absence of unfettered access by UN inspectors, neither the UN nor anyone else was likely to find out the true situation, until it was too late. Why the UN, and in particular core and influential members such as France, Germany and Russia, resisted taking what, by any standards, was the only meaningful way forward, is slowly coming to light with the emergence of the UN scandal over the administration of the 'oil-for-food' programme and the massive potential financial loss that would be sustained, particularly by French business interests, along with Russian and German ones. Given that the UN's programme was the single largest humanitarian effort in human history (with an enormous associated cost of tens of billions), the magnitude of this potential scandal (at the time of writing the extent of it is still being investigated) and the billions of French investments at risk, may well go a long way to revealing why some Western nations were quite prepared to connive with Saddam's international defiance — and thus with the aims of international terrorists.

What emerges from a more objective review of the evidence is that this was not a 'Second War', as some would have it. Nor is the lack of discovery of WMD particularly significant. The problem was not that they definitely existed anyway. The problem was that no one was able to confirm the fact one way or the other without force. I have little doubt personally that caches of WMD may exist and that they may yet be found in some bunker in Iraq, or more likely housed just across the border in neighbouring, Saddam-friendly, Syria. A recent find of Sarin and mustard gas[3] by the Americans near that border suggests a much larger cache somewhere. The mistake Tony Blair made — and one partially avoided by President Bush, who moved early from justifying the war on strictly WMD grounds to promoting the need for regime change — was to keep insisting that they *would* be found, and soon. Tony Blair acted courageously in this matter (and I am no fan of Tony Blair's politics generally) by supporting the Americans in doing the right thing in this instance when the UN, largely influenced by France, shamefully refused to do so. Because of his insistence over WMD, however, Mr Blair brought unnecessary pressure on himself.

The fact is that the USA and the UK did not lie to its peoples, and neither did the West's intelligence communities. The CIA's head of intelligence, George Tenet, reportedly told his president that the presence of WMD in Saddam's Iraq at the beginning of 2003 was a 'slam dunk'.[4] This was the reality of all the intelligence they were receiving, albeit in some cases from dubious sources. Add this to the light of the evidence we have already articulated, and the whole post-war debate over WMD appears thoroughly misconceived and wrong-headed. The fact is that Saddam had WMD, used them, and was still obsessed with acquiring them. The fact is that he had links with al-Qu'eda and international terrorism. It was Saddam's highly duplicitous behaviour in keeping 'full and final' information concerning his alleged possession of WMD from the UN which, in the end, expedited his own downfall. The UN's own reports all bear this out. The reality is this: whether he managed to hide WMD by getting them out of the country prior to the invasion, or whether he simply 'dug a hole' for them somewhere, or indeed whether every single WMD was destroyed, is *all entirely irrelevant. What is relevant is that the UN was never able to verify the true position one way or another.* Am I missing something here? Or is much of the hand-wringing of the Western media and political elites over the lack of WMD post-invasion merely so much 'hot air' and entirely unworthy of so many column inches?

If we are realistic and not idealistic, the invasion was not only justified but fundamentally necessary if the UN was to retain any degree of credibility in brokering ceasefire situations at the end of wars. If it will not instigate its own resolutions, it appears that someone else may have to do so for them, if evil despots like Saddam are not to run rings around them and the will of the international community generally.

Whatever problems Iraq experienced after the invasion, either through coalition mishandling or increased terrorist activity (desperate to prevent real democracy taking hold), these are entirely separate matters which cannot deflect from the honourable nature of the US-led cause. The role of the USA and the UK and their allies in pursuing much needed regime change in Iraq was both ethical and noble. Women in Iraq are free as never before. Already, within a year, there are more schools open, more electricity is flowing, more revenue-producing oil is pumping than ever before. The population no longer lives in dread of a regime where the daily injustices, maiming and murdering, were a way of life. But, above all, Saddam's evil regime and his obsessive pursuit of WMD have been dealt a deathblow. The reason for all of the post-war violence, on the other hand, is straightforward enough. The Islamist militants cannot possibly allow this potential exercise in the introduction of true democracy to work, whether the majority of Iraq's population wish it or not. They know only too well the problems it will cause in other Islamic and Arab countries if it does succeed and prosper the Iraqi people — and right on their doorstep. That is why they are desperate to go to the lengths that they have to prevent the emergence of a new democratic Iraq, where women are free and where education teaches truth and not Islamofascist propaganda.

In all of this, one question needs to be asked of the West's liberals and all of those who have opposed the war and attacked the US and UK administrations for executing it: 'Explain, if you can, *your* argument for why *you* say Saddam Hussein should still be in power in Iraq?' The truth is, it is not the role of the US-led coalition and the issue of WMD that ought to be the public and media obsession. It ought to be the shrinking, timorous and baffling conduct of the inept and ineffective UN for twelve years prior to invasion. New information is, even as I write, coming to light and answering previously dark and puzzling questions concerning the UN's role in Iraq. But before we address further the troubling subject of the activities of the UN in these events, let us address the issue of Saddam's very real and *still existing* WMD (and the mystery of its disappeared airforce) and *exactly* where it is today.

So *exactly* where are Saddam's WMD?

The reason that the USA-led coalition has not found large stockpiles of Saddam's WMD is twofold. First, in the face of the pressure of having to move them around to keep them from the prying eyes of the UN inspectors, 'Saddam moved virtually all production capabilities to Libya and Sudan somewhere between 1996 and 1998' and 'subsequently in 2002' (with invasion looking odds-on) 'the residual chemical weapons production capabilities were shipped to Iran where they were stored in two clusters of tunnels under the Zagros Mountains...some 15-20 miles from the Iraqi border'.[5] The fact that Saddam was at war with Iran in the 1980s should not divert the reader from understanding the duplicity of the Iranian mullahs in doing what best serves their own longer-term interests, especially faced with their 'horror' at the prospect of a USA-friendly government on their border.

Second, on the very eve of the invasion itself — and, at the very time the USA and the UK had bowed to pressure to go back to the United Nations to make one last attempt to get an agreement for joint UN-sponsored enforcement — Saddam took the opportunity of the further respite to remove the last vestiges of his stockpile of WMD into Syria and Syrian-sponsored Lebanon, and its chemical warheads

The Politics of Faith

into North Korea, along with many Iraqi planes, to keep them away from 'international eyes'.[6] Indeed, other reports reveal, 'In December 2002, Iraq began moving its WMD — its weapons, research and manufacturing equipment, records, and personnel — out of Iraq to Syria and Lebanon.'[7] Saddam's men were still moving Saddam's his store of WMD, according to a number of reports, right up to the siege of Baghdad itself. Ironically, at the very time the 'coalition of the willing' would have been able to catch Saddam with the famed 'smoking gun' of WMD, the US/UK-led coalition found itself once again bogged down in the quagmire of endless and fruitless UN discussions that were always destined to go nowhere. As the destination of Saddam's WMD arsenal becomes more widely known (as it surely will), not doubt it will be seen that it was the very procrastination of the UN, along with the insistent voices of the liberal lobbies demanding UN 'legitimacy' (when the forum of the UN is dominated by the paralysis of self-interest), which meant that the coalition forces were ultimately denied the prospect of catching Saddam red-handed.

Just as disturbing, however, was the complete failure of the intelligence — and particularly the US intelligence agencies — to provide the Bush administration with much better information on the true picture in Iraq. For a start, the fact that much of Saddam's WMD capability had been transferred out of Iraq in the mid-90s was well-known to parts of US intelligence. For example, as far back as 1998, the Task Force on Terrorism and Unconventional Warfare of the US House of Representatives issued a report citing that 'the hard core of Saddam Hussein's primary WMD development and production programmes...are run outside of Iraq — mainly in Sudan and Libya, as well as Algeria.'[8] Such an extraordinary 'corporate memory'[9] lapse of the US intelligence community amounted to nothing less than 'a colossal failure of intelligence that subjected the [Bush] administration to an unnecessary political embarrassment and humiliation'.[10] This in turn has meant that 'opposing politicians and the media have used the failure to discover WMD as a political weapon against the Bush administration, but the real culprits are in the intelligence communities.'[11]

The responsibility for the failure to act sooner and enforce UN resolutions which would have turned up the 'smoking gun' that the world sought, must of course remain firmly at the door of the UN — and those at the UN who sought to tie the hands of the nations who recognized that the time for action was well overdue. And chief among the ringleaders is France. If we needed any evidence of the culpability of Jacques Chirac's devious double-dealing government, then we should look no further than the chosen location of many of Saddam's thugs and henchmen after the March 2003 invasion — Paris — and, not least, the *reason* for that choice of (protective) destination.

> Another favorite destination among Iraqi VIPs was Paris. The first group sent there — made up of scientists and spies — was flown to France from Damascus on the night of April 14 and provided with French travel documents by the embassy in Damascus. Essentially, Paris determined to hide from Washington's view the Iraqis who knew anything about the extent of French co-operation with Saddam on any number of sensitive issues — from nuclear technology to Iraqi campaign contributions to prominent French politicians. (These arrangements have been described by several sources, and in the French book *Our Friend Saddam*.)[12]

Which brings us back to the real scandal highlighted by the invasion of Iraq in 2003.

The scandal of the United Nations

In April 2004 a scandal broke, the reverberations of which threaten to rock the UN — and the world's perception of it — to its very foundations. Though, at the time of writing, the UN is still investigating itself through nine separate inquiry bodies, it is clear that billions of dollars from the UN's oil-for-food programme, destined to feed the children and dependants of Iraq, were diverted into the pockets of Saddam Hussein personally — *with the full knowledge of UN member states and officials.* According to *The Daily Telegraph's* headline, quoting from a report to the US Congress, 'UN officials covered up Saddam's theft of billions in aid for Iraqis'.[13] The bottom line of the allegation is that it was achieved with the connivance of 'senior UN, French and Russian officials', according to Claude Hankes-Drielsma, former leader of the Iraqi Governing Council who was conducting a post-war Iraqi enquiry into the affair which undoubtedly allowed Saddam to use the money to 'buy influence' around the world.

Hankes-Drielsma was well placed to have identified the scandal. He had been a leading executive at the London-based auditors Price Waterhouse. Investigating the operation of the oil-for-food programme as chairman of Roland Berger UK, Hankes-Drielsma wrote to the UN on a number of occasions, urging the need for an independent investigation.[14] He received no reply from the UN. As Mr Hankes-Drielsma later told the US Congress, 'The very fact that Saddam Hussein, the UN and certain members of the Security Council could conceal such a scam from the world should send shivers down every spine in this room'.[15]

It ought to be remembered that the oil-for-food programme was the biggest humanitarian scheme in UN history. It is currently alleged that the man responsible for actually operating the UN programme, Benon Sevan, personally pocketed substantial bribes. At the time of writing

Mr Sevan is on 'extended leave with a view to early retirement'.[16] Sevan has made little attempt to deny the allegations. Others named in one report to the US Congress were identical to names in a similar report drawn up by post-war Iraqi investigators. They included 'the office of President Putin of Russia'[17], the French Interior Minister Jean-Bernard Merimee, and a host of others. Most of the oil-for-food programme funds passed through French banks where

> some of the money was siphoned off to bribe high-ranking French politicians, possibly including President Chirac. French banks handled nearly $50 billion in Oil-for-Food transactions, and anyone who believes the French — or the Russians, the Germans, the Jordanians, the Syrians, and the rest — will be forthcoming with documentation and witnesses essential to the [UN] investigation is dreaming. Thus, it will be impossible for the Annan-appointed investigators to uncover the evidence necessary to reveal the culpability of the UN, or many of its culpable members and staff.[18]

The USA and Britain had repeatedly protested to the UN about oil-smuggling and other abuses, to no avail. But no one, not even the governments of the USA and UK, appeared to be aware of the sheer magnitude of what was going on — and how UN funds were being channelled to aid international terrorism.

Some of the specifics of what is being alleged, as the *Telegraph* reported, are that 'some suppliers, mostly Russian, routinely sent out-of-date or unfit food, or sent fewer goods than were paid for, and padded out contracts. In that way they created an excess that could be skimmed off by Iraqi officials'.[19] The oil-for-food programme ran from 1995 until 2003 and was designed to allow Iraq legally to export oil worth billions of pounds despite UN sanctions, so that children and other vulnerable members of the population could receive food and medicine. The fact that this burgeoning scandal involves high-ranking UN, Russian and French officials, among others, should speak volumes as to their preferred mode of dealing with the errant Iraqi leadership — effectively neutralizing entirely the role of the UN. These billions of pounds represented the money of Western taxpayers aiding the sick, poor and vulnerable in pre-war Iraq. Yet, for seven years, the UN programme ran virtually without serious scrutiny. As if this scandal itself is not enough, it begs the much deeper question: is this why the UN, dominated by a Franco-Russian-Germanic block, was so inert and unwilling for twelve years to take any meaningful action in support of its own resolutions against Saddam's Iraq? If we couple all of this to the fact of enormous French business interests in pre-2003 Iraq, the relentless opposition of Jacques Chirac, and the French propensity for political self-interest, the reason becomes all too apparent.

Even though an Iraqi opposition delegation travelled to New York in January 2003 to ask specifically for a Security Council investigation and audit[20] into Saddam's massive abuse of the programme, the UN Security Council refused to act. And when the story did finally break in the press in the Spring of 2004, the response of the UN was to write to all of those companies involved in the programme, calling upon them not to release any documentation to the media until they, the UN, had vetted it.

It is ironic, is it not, that the chief outcry against the US-led mission has been that it did not first seek (though latterly Tony Blair did make approaches) the unifying force of a UN mandate before finally moving to impose the will of the international community upon Saddam. But, as this scandal reveals, and as the Americans knew well enough, the UN, and specifically France, Russia and Germany, for self-serving reasons, would *never* have sanctioned it. It appears that there was just too much at stake for the nations who most love playing political chess, using the UN as a powerful pawn to sustain their own private interests.

When the people of Iraq vote for their new democratic government early in 2005, they will have the allied 'coalition of the willing' to thank for it, and not the distinctly unwilling and morally bankrupt UN, French and Russian governments and a large swathe of humanitarian liberals who believe in appeasement and not enforcement. If the latter had had their way, Saddam would still be in power. He would still be murdering and torturing his own people. But, most of all, he would still be pursuing (and eventually succeeding) in his obsession for WMD — and still 'tweaking the nose' of the UN and the international community in that pursuit. Only Western liberals could keep bleating about WMD in the face of all of this evidence. Only Western liberals could perceive the invasion and regime change in Iraq as anything other than for the greater good — and, more specifically, welcome to the overwhelming majority of 25 million Iraqis. It is not the province of the UN, or its cosy coterie of socialist Western nations, to decide the morality of right action. Moral fibre is, after all, more often than not the province of the few rather than the many. It was God, the Bible tells us, who 'set the nations' in their place. We should not therefore share the UN's patent disdain for the nation-state[21], but rather maintain God's empowerment of it.

A footnote for Christians

The secular case, if we as Christians wish to call it that, for the invasion of Iraq ought to be plain enough when the evidence is viewed objectively. Why is it then that the world's liberals have as vociferous 'bedfellows' many in leadership in the modern church? Well, it could easily have something to do with the fact that the present church leadership is itself professedly liberal and non-biblical in its prevailing worldview, as I have shown elsewhere.[22] Much of what passes for modern Christianity has been given a lead by the liberal-dominated thinking which is 'anti-war' (forgetting that there is such a Bible-sanctioned act as the 'just war') and 'anti-the taking of life' (when the Bible plainly sanctions the death penalty — see 'Saddam and the Death Penalty' in this volume — and judicial killing). This sets up a climate of theoretic and academic rhetoric for the armchair 'theologians' to pontificate on esoteric, humanly devised philosophies to their heart's content. The bottom line is that, while their 'anti-war' stances allow them to appear somehow more spiritual, ultimately their esoteric, professorial ramblings have little to do with acting in the real world. Marching, and making popular rhetoric against *any* form of armed conflict or *any* matters involving the taking of human life, after all, is easy, and too often what liberal (non-biblical) 'churchy' people do best. But it is not real, biblical Christianity. Liberal 'churchy' people are often theoretic pacifists who have little trouble holding the morally abhorrent position of being 'anti-death penalty' when it comes to taking the life of guilty mass murderers, but 'pro-choice' — a mere euphemism when it comes to killing innocent children in the womb. But, just as we cannot depend upon them to apply the Scriptures in almost any other area of life, neither should we expect them to make any valuable proper contribution on behalf of the Christian church on such matters as the invasion of Iraq or other world affairs.

I have also heard that some Christians have tried to make out a case for denouncing any invasion of a *sovereign* nation, as God set all of the nations in place (as indeed he did). But if that were the case, was it right for the Second World War allies to cross the borders into Germany and pursue regime change in that nation? If this argument stands up, then it could not have been. But why is it that the Bible records numerous occasions when God specifically raised up one nation to 'chastise' others, to remind them of the extent of their unrepented national and private sins? Israel and Judah were continually occupied by foreign powers whom God raised up to teach 'his children' a lesson in godly humility.

If we are looking for an appropriate Bible teaching to bring to bear on the situation in Iraq pre-2003, it ought not to be those verses which speak of sovereign nationhood (though even if it were, what of Iraq's 'excursions' into Iran and Kuwait?). Far more appropriate is speaking of 'loving our neighbours' and 'resisting evil', perhaps. Or are we simply content to allow the mass murder of Iraqi citizens and the invasion of neighbouring nations to go on under Saddam's regime? The truth is, with the ineptitude and corruption of the UN, the US-led coalition was the only real moral 'game in town'. That is if the long-suffering people of Iraq were going to receive the aid, liberation and freedom that so many craved — and not have their private agonies extended humiliatingly by the unending 'games' being played out between their evil president and a corrupt UN.

Who showed real 'love' in these circumstances; which nations 'gave' of themselves, in terms of the giving of their lives for others, will all be recorded as facts of history. It will also tell us that the liberation of Iraq in 2003 was not a 'second war' at all, but rather a resumption of the 1991 Gulf War after the terms of the ceasefire continued to be broken by Saddam. Ultimately, in the light of Saddam's scorn for the world community and for the plight of his own people for more than twelve years — with the many deaths and the suffering that has been brought about — the moral right in this case has been more than made out, WMD or no WMD.

'Greater love hath no man than to lay down his life for his friends.' I believe history will show — and that eternity will reveal to Christians — that the invasion of Iraq in 2003 *was* the moral and noble thing to have done, for all the failings of the 'coalition of the willing', both pre- and post-war, in God's cosmic scheme of things.

---

[1] I was a national spokesman for the Crown Prosecution Service in the UK and Public Relations Officer to the Director of Public Prosecutions for three years in the early 90s.

[2] Which has, in my view, unnecessarily got him into hot water. When the Americans had the good sense to speak of the need for regime change as well as WMD, Tony Blair continued to insist that 'WMD would be found given time'. Given the fact, as it now appears, that Western intelligence agencies were misled, and that it is perfectly possible that some are still in a hole in the ground somewhere or, more likely, in Syria, one wonders why Blair stuck rigidly to the one line, inviting criticism upon himself. I am not sure whether this is due to poor PR advice on the part of advisors, or to his own perception of how to handle the affair.

[3] These are WMD. They were found in late Spring 2004 in relatively small quantities. The anti-war BBC and the British media generally did not even bother to report these finds.

[4] Reported by author Bob Woodward in *Plan of Attack: The Road to War* (New York: Simons & Schuster, 2004).

[5] Yossef Bodansky (director of the Congressional Task Force on Terrorism and Unconventional Warfare and former director of research at the International Strategic Studies Association and senior editor for the Defense and Foreign Affairs Group of publications), *The Secret History of the Iraq War* (New York: Regan Books, 2004) p. 496.

[6] ibid. pp.438-9. How it was achieved, who was involved (including the personal complicity of Syrian president Bashir Assar) and where exactly the WMD resided post-2003 are all set out here in explicit detail. Bodansky notes that Assad's agreement to store this material was predicated upon his belief that the USA would not risk the further wrath of the Arab nations by attacking Syria as well. He was right.

[7] Jed Babbin, *Inside The Asylum: Why The United Nations and Old Europe are Worse Than You Think* (New York: Regnery, 2004), p. 34. Jed Babbin is the former Deputy Undersecretary of Defense for the USA.

8 'The Iraqi WMD Challenge – Myths and Reality', The Task Force on Terrorism and Unconventional Warfare, 10 February 1998.

9 Bodansky, op. cit., p. 497.

10 Bodansky, op. cit., p.497.

11 Bodansky, op. cit., p.500.

12 Bodansky, op. cit., p.262.

13 *The Daily Telegraph*, Thursday 22 April 2004.

14 In one letter to the UN marked 'Urgent' Hankes-Drielsma wrote 'Indications are that not less than 10% was added to the value of all invoices to provide cash to Saddam Hussein (as much as £4 billion). If so, why was this not identified and prevented? Was the UN alerted to this at any stage? What action was taken and who was made aware of this allegation?' – reported by Jed Babbin, op.cit., p. 151.

15 'UN officials "covered up Saddam's theft of billions in aid for Iraqis" ', *The Daily Telegraph*, Thursday 22 April 2004.

16 ibid.

17 ibid.

18 Babbin, op. cit., p. 30.

19 *The Daily Telegraph*, op. cit.

20 Report in 'The UN's Money Trail' in *World* magazine, 1 May 2004.

21 'In 1996, senator Jesse Helms of North Carolina sounded an urgent warning about the UN: The international elites running the United Nations look at the idea of the nation-state with disdain; they consider it a discredited notion of the past that has been superseded by the idea of the United Nations. In their view the interests of the nation-states are parochial and should give way to the global interests. Nation-states, they believe, should recognize the primacy of these global interests and accede to the United Nations' sovereignty to pursue them'. Babbin, op. cit., pp.81-2.

22 See my book *The Virtual Church – and how to avoid it': The Crisis of De-formation and the Need for Re-formation in the 21st Century Church* (Florida: Xulon Press, 2004).

4
Who Killed David Kelly?

Let me be clear from the start. This essay adduces no homespun theories concerning the death of former Government weapons inspector David Kelly. Who killed David Kelly is, as far as this writer is concerned, clear enough: David Kelly killed David Kelly. Greatly disturbed by his sudden notoriety in the Iraqi War weapons of mass destruction (WMD) affair, he ended up taking a knife he had had since he was five years old and, along with an overdose of drugs, took a final walk to his death in July 2003. Nobody, neither the coroner nor the local police, nor any sensible person familiar with the evidence, seriously questions that Dr Kelly took this walk for the purpose of committing suicide in a local wood.

But who, in the general scheme of things, was to be blamed for the brewing of a situation which would result in a prominent leading scientist ending his time thus? Where *exactly* ought the responsibility to lie for this tragic state of affairs that culminated in Kelly's death? The theories have flowed thick and fast. The nuanced accusations against politicians and the media have been innumerable. Internet websites have been set up to feed the nutty-fringe 'conspiracy theory' officianados, and so on. But in all of this, the only issue which appears to have escaped closer scrutiny is that which deals with the area of personal responsibility when it comes to the morality of 'self-murder' and its effects. And, in reviewing this, the whole issue of personal moral responsibility generally comes more fully into perspective and focus. Because it was plainly David Kelly who, when all the evidence is weighed, was responsible for creating the ultimately crushing pressure and stress — and for ending it by taking the drastic action he did.

Why then was the subsequent media inquest into his death focused almost exclusively on apportioning the blame for this series of events to just about everyone, from the Prime Minister to senior MOD officials, to the security forces and the media; indeed to anyone except the one solely ultimately responsible for it: David Kelly himself? What the ensuing media debate highlighted, if anything, is the contemporary penchant for blaming one's own sins on anyone and everyone else.

In the media spat between the Government and the BBC, and the general rush to express regret and praise for Kelly's laudable long-term service to his country, I cannot recollect a single voice lamenting the fact that, in taking the deeply self-centred and cowardly direction of suicide, Kelly hardly fitted the media profile of the 'devoted husband', 'loving father' and 'caring family man'. After all, having told his wife that he was 'off for a walk' when he was off to commit suicide, he was revealing himself as a man so preoccupied with himself and his own problems that he had no compunction whatever in leaving his family to suffer the personal trauma and psychological scars of his loss and of his cowardly, self-centred, action. It is hard to see how a man who was truly caring, loving and devoted could ever do such a terrible thing to those nearest and dearest to him. After all, it was merely a 'loss of face' which he believed himself to be suffering; he was not in serious life-threatening danger or at risk of prison. The truth is his final decisions were all about private ego and not about concern for those around him. It seems, as with all suicide 'victims', that self-love and ego, if unchecked, in the end easily vanquish love for our fellow man, or even our closest loved ones. But then the fact that Kelly's personal culpability in this matter has been almost exclusively missed by a media and political campaign so hung up on their own private agendas, that the issue of personal morality a recurring characteristic of the current 'me, me' generation has been entirely obfuscated. Dr David Kelly may well have thought that he was ridding himself of all the burdens of life on that 'dark' July day in 2003, but he was in fact surely only *adding* to the burdens of the family he left behind — possibly for the rest of their lives. If Dr Kelly's love for them had been as great as was painted, then the very thought of distressing those around him by committing suicide, and thereby taking the 'easy' way out, would have caused him far more concern, and surely deflected him from the course he eventually took.

We know that Kelly, four years previously, had become a member of the Ba'hai faith (a religion which denies the right to suicide) even though both he and his wife were members, apparently, of the Anglican Church. All that we may surmise from these two facts, however, is that he had 'vague' spiritual leanings which, when 'push came to shove', made very little difference to him. This is, of course, evidence that however Kelly saw his own spirituality, ultimately it had little real effect upon him, as both religions deny the right to suicide and in the case of the Christian faith, with severe 'heavenly' consequences for those who commit premeditated murder, even self-murder.

When the Hutton Report investigation into David Kelly's suicide eventually emerged in January 2004, it concluded that it 'could not have been predicted' by anyone. Its findings also provide us with an insight into an 'intensely private man' and, tellingly perhaps, into the fact that he was 'not an easy man to help or to whom to give advice'. It seems that Dr Kelly had become increasingly depressed by what Lord Hutton called a 'fear of public disgrace'. This depression is understandable, given Kelly's life of public service and with 'great distinction' for his country. What had so disturbed the whole course of his life now, however, was that he had been publicly outed as the source of a headline story by the BBC; a story which actually accused the Prime Minister of the day of *knowingly* lying to Parliament and the people of the United Kingdom by providing 'spiced up' intelligence reports on the nature of WMD in Iraq, in order to gain support for a military campaign to depose Saddam's thuggish regime. The furore surrounding this serious and potentially defamatory accusation against the Government was perhaps unsurprising, given the allegations. Neither was the hunt for the 'source' of the BBC's story going to go away. As all parties have conceded, it was inevitable that the BBC's source would, one way or another, be made public. Knowing he was the source of that story, and having been placed in an impossible position the BBC having been somewhat cavalier with its broadcast 'interpretation' of what he had said to them the pressure upon David Kelly was building as soon as the BBC's iconic Radio Four *Today* programme aired it.

In his report into the causes which led up to David Kelly committing suicide, Lord Hutton concluded that the BBC's broadcast accusation was in fact based on faulty information and was thus false. The BBC reporter who publicly made the allegation, Andrew Gilligan, the Hutton enquiry revealed, had based his accusation on notes of an interview with Kelly which did not corroborate or support the accusation he had actually made: that the Prime Minister had intentionally lied to the country in order to take it into the Iraq War. In the face of such an allegation potentially bringing down the government, the Prime Minister's response was both swift and angry. One would have thought that all the BBC and Gilligan needed to do, given what the Hutton report later found to be the case concerning Gilligan's plainly inadequate notes, was to issue an immediate apology and resolve the matter forthwith. But it was in the mealy-mouthed procrastination of Gilligan and his BBC bosses that the whole matter blew up into a scandal which would run for a full seven months, with accusations flying on every hand. Meanwhile the pain of potential, almost inevitable, public disgrace was taking its toll on David Kelly, who, realizing he was caught between a 'rock and a hard place', with his credibility about to be shredded by public exposure coupled with the BBC's misuse of his information, could see the value of his life's work being washed away in a single tide. It was this, above all, which appears to have led him to take his fateful final decision. While no one for a moment suggests that the situation was not a desperately depressing and painful one for him, it is asserted here that our sympathy for him should expire at the point where he believed that taking his own life was the only path open to him, and that in doing so he was affecting only himself and hurting no one else.

It is in the aftermath of the deed that it became clear that everyone rushed to praise Kelly and blame just about everyone else, including absurdly and totally unfairly Prime Minister Tony Blair, for that which Kelly had ultimately brought upon himself. In this we may perceive the increasing lack of logic and perversity in much modern thinking. For whichever way we cut this particular 'cake', the unalterable linear facts of the matter are these:

1. Dr Kelly set the whole ball rolling *himself* when he made the decision to break the terms of his employment with the Ministry of Defence and discuss with a national journalist matters of restricted national

security and intelligence pertaining to Iraqi WMD. (I understand this situation only too well as a former public relations officer for the Director of Public Prosecutions.)

2. Unfortunately, he eventually agreed to speak to the BBC's Andrew Gilligan, a journalist who, as it turns out, was less than careful with the critical information given to him; a man who was singularly responsible for helping to blow up a modern day mini-scandal and a man whose reporting was later described by a BBC editor as 'marred by flawed journalism'.

3. Gilligan, using sparse notes from his interview with Kelly, was himself interviewed by the BBC's *Today* programme anchor, John Humphries. In that interview Gilligan effectively accused the Prime Minister of the day of purposely lying to the nation in presenting 'sexed up' details of intelligence reports on WMD in Iraq, to Parliament and to the country and did so solely on the basis of his single source, the notes he took when interviewing David Kelly. Such an assertion was rightly viewed as extremely serious in Government circles, as well as by the rest of the media.

4. In the internal investigation which followed the broadcast, the BBC programme editors, so it transpired, failed to check Gilligan's notes for themselves (as they did before his broadcast). Neither did the Director-General Greg Dyke, nor, ultimately, the BBC Board of Governors, check them after the interview was aired. All consequently 'stood by' their journalist's story on his word alone, a position they held for a *full* seven months.

5. When the Hutton Report was published, it showed that Gilligan's notes by Gilligan's own admission — did *not* bear out or support in any way the accusation

he himself had made. Essentially, the story was found to be false and unsubstantiated, even according to his 'source' notes.

6. In short, Dr Kelly began the whole fiasco by breaking his own terms of employment and speaking to a journalist about national security matters; the journalist he spoke to was not of the highest calibre; and that journalist eventually dropped him 'in it' by making false accusations on public radio, accusations which actually misrepresented much of what Kelly had told him.

Quite clearly, Dr Kelly had nobody but himself, and a less-than-accurate BBC journalist, to blame for the distress he subsequently found himself suffering. He knew he was Gilligan's 'source'. He knew he would be named. He could not face the ignominy of the public disgrace. It was all too much for a man whose ego was such that what mattered above all else was avoiding the public disgrace — not how much love he had for his family.

Many people, including a building full of BBC journalists, subsequently took to the street complaining about 'Government bullying' of the 'free media'. Yet those same journalists would certainly have called for the heads of Government employees had the situation been reversed. Surely, it is then only right that those who failed to 'come clean' at the BBC, thus feeding the media frenzy by their own ineptitude and for seven months — and thereby by ratcheting up the threshold of anticipatory exposure for the tragic David Kelly — should pay a price for their duplicity, as they eventually did with senior dismissals and the 'departure' of Gilligan himself. It is indeed right that the national press and media ought to be free to report, but they also ought to be responsible and answerable for the truth of what they report.

In all of this, however, one of the worrying characteristics of the whole affair remains, as we have seen here, the distinct lack of concern for the personal rights and responsibilities surrounding suicide, as if it were of no consequence at all. And yet for the heart to contemplate suicide is for the heart to contemplate murder, albeit self-murder, when all is said and done. David Kelly, to his credit, sought physically to hurt no one but himself. But as a created human being, he callously chose to scar and leave behind those he claimed to love, being more concerned for himself and his own egotistical 'loss of face' than for those around him. That Lord Hutton found him a man 'to whom it was not easy to give advice' and that he certainly did not understand the true nature of faith to which he allegedly laid claim, will not help one iota when it comes to answering for his crime: not merely that of breaking his MOD employment rules, but the far more serious one of committing murder, albeit 'self-murder', when he comes to answer before a higher court than that of public opinion.

ISSUE: values & politics in the media

5
The Liberal Bias of the Media

I have long since given up expecting honest, old-fashioned, balanced news reporting from the BBC. Nor are the rest of the British broadcast media and much of the serious print media much better — at least when it comes to reporting on political and social issues. The reason is quite simple: what is thought of as 'balanced' and 'mainstream' media reporting in the UK has, for some time, been nothing of the sort. As a long-time observer and monitor of news reporting on both sides of the Atlantic, I can say that the situation in the USA is not much better. The only difference is that media observers in the USA are at least alive to their situation. Indeed in the USA it is the subject of much public and media debate as well as the subject of much published literature. Back in the motherland, however, ever maintaining the steadfast self-delusion that we have free speech, the more conservative media consumer is still gently snoozing, secure in the belief that the latest political and social news report is being presented untainted by creed, propaganda and, heaven forbid, blatant untruth.

The Politics of Faith

Is our media WSYWYG (what you see is what you get)?
That both countries have evolved a liberal media bias which is consistently skewing the majority of current affairs reports, and thus the court of public opinion, ought to be known to us and a matter of great concern. But for something to concern us, we first have to be alert to the problem. The assertion of liberal media bias in America, with the majority of the broadcast and print media expressing increasingly uniform partisan views over issues such as the Iraq War, the place of the death penalty, abortion, the disciplining of children and so on, has led directly to the creation of a conservative news channel, Fox News. Today Fox just happens to be the most watched cable channel TV news (I would say with good reason), bearing out the central assertion of this article that mainstream media cannot be trusted to handle the news with sufficient, non-partisan equity. Fox News was set up specifically to counterbalance the prevailing anti-Americanism across the mainstream US media generally. This event was the corollary to a general awakening of consumers increasingly aware of the inherent anti-conservatism which (as numerous Gallup and other polls revealed) was a long way from reflecting and expressing their own views. It is simple enough to detect precisely the same divergence of moral views expressed by and in the media from those more widely held by a conservative-minded populace, though perhaps less markedly so in the UK than in the States.

It seems that the romantic notion of a 'brave wartime' BBC, free from dogma and ever intent on presenting truth and not propaganda, still persists among the British public — against all the evidence. Bunkum. It really is time that the British public woke up to the fact that their daily morning and evening news is (and has been for some time) serving them up a steady diet of politically-correct liberalism which, more often than not, *opposes* rather than *reflects* the views of the often more conservative-minded viewer and listener. Indeed the whole 'playing field' in the UK is clouded by the self-deluding nonsense that we are neither a British culture nor a predominantly Christian nation (at least nominally), but rather a multi-cultural, multi-faith society. In its attempts to divest itself of its national identity, this is a 'horse' which not only 'won't run', but would (and rightly so) be flogged to death at the starting gate in most other nations.

If you want an insight into what I am talking about here, read *The Spectator* for a few weeks. It rejoices in its *raison d'être* as an organ prepared to publish articles from any shade of politics and worldview, just so long as they are well argued. As a consequence, its pages typically juxtapose the leftist, anti-American, anti-Iraq War, pro-liberal agendas of the likes of Stephen Glover (*no* relation!), Rod Liddle and 'let's-not-let-the-facts-get-in-the-way-of-a-good-story' former BBC journalist Andrew Gilligan, alongside conservative writers like William Shawcross, Charles Moore and the 'a-little-to-the-right-of-Attila-the Hun-inspired' jottings of Mark Steyn (for my money, the best of the bunch). I have no problem with this. We all know where everyone is coming from and why. It is plain and out in the open. But this is my whole point. Just like the apostle Paul, I have no problem with a free marketplace of ideas (something *The Spectator* wears as its badge of honour). Truth has a persistent habit of 'rising to the surface' in such a climate. I have every problem, however, with a marketplace bearing a multiplicity of labels but essentially selling the same basic postmodern goods where absolute truth, moral superiority and the higher communal good are all conspicuous by their absence.

So where is the evidence of liberal bias?
Even a snapshot assessment of some of the coverage of the key issues of the day reveals something of the extent of liberal media bias. Why, for instance, when the general

conservatively-minded population is so consistently *pro-death penalty*, is the mainstream media almost exclusively dismissive and disdainful of public opinion?[1] And, in a democracy, by what right anyway? When was the last time you were even 'allowed' to read a well-written case for the death penalty in a major media publication? Why does the mainstream media insist on its default position which presents those in favour of abortion on demand as 'pro-choice' and 'fair-minded', while characterizing those who oppose it as 'anti-choice' and illiberal zealots?

Why is it that when the majority of Brits so widely oppose EU federal integration, the media consistently gives the Europhile case more airtime[2], with soundbite after soundbite asserting that Europhiles simply 'need to get their case across better' (implying the public is in ignorance) while Eurosceptics are depicted as a ramshackle anti-intellectual bunch of 'anti-Europeans' (rather than what they actually are, i.e. anti-European Unionists).

Why does the mainstream media continue to assert that the homosexual community is more substantial in number than it actually is, representing its case as not only a human rights issue but one where the rest of society should positively affirm its cause as 'moral'?[3] Why do so many broadcast and print journalists relentlessly persist in pressing the case which denies Britain's Christian heritage by insisting it adopt an anti-British, anti-Christian, multi-cultural, and multi-faith stance (i.e. with no culture or faith predominating)?

And why[4] has the mainstream media been so pervasively anti-American and anti-Iraq War in presenting its case to the British people — laced with an ever-present hostility to George W. Bush? At the same time, why has the media reported almost nothing of the growing 'oil-for-food' scandal which undoubtedly, so it seems, will prove to be the chief reason why the Franco-Russian-influenced UN refused to take any action against Saddam's regime although it had flouted all of the UN's 17 post-1991 War resolutions.[5] Yet, when the USA-led alliance, after 12 years of suffering Saddam's 'nose-thumbing', world-defying activities, enforced the UN's resolutions, the liberal media took the side, as it is now being shown, of a corrupt Franco-Russian-United Nations unholy alliance. Why, for instance, has the massive rebuilding programme for schools, hospitals and infrastructure in Iraq been totally overlooked and unreported by the British media? Why has the news been ignored (suppressed?) that more Iraqi citizens now have electricity and that Iraq is today pumping more oil, and producing more revenue for itself, than under previous regimes? Do not misunderstand what I am saying here. I do not ask for the media to change its anti-war stance, merely that they tell something of the fuller truth. I have heard countless stories of Americans and Iraqis arriving back in the USA, only to be stunned by the one-sided nature of the Western liberal media's coverage. By any standards, ours appears to be a media with an agenda bent on presenting an utterly false impression of an Iraq in chaos, when it is not.

As someone who has spent many years working in and monitoring the mainstream media in both the UK and the USA, perhaps I have the advantage over the average imbiber of mainstream news channels in the UK. At least I know where to go to find more balanced and fairer news which dilutes and balances the rhetoric of the liberal-dominated British media.

In the light of the appalling BBC journalism which led to the suicide of Government scientist David Kelly[6] after the publication of Lord Hutton's damning indictment of journalistic standards at the BBC, we have at least been formally alerted to the increasingly poor standards of slanted journalism. Even after the Hutton Report, further leaks of internal BBC memos reveal that journalistic concerns by senior BBC executives over the 'climate of sloppiness', 'unvetted stories', 'littered with errors, inaccurate and potentially libellous' and general 'shoddy journalism' remain unabated.[7] If for no other reason, the public should be concerned because it is taxpayers' money which pays for the BBC through the compulsory licence fee system.

Neither does one have to look far these days for the consistent litany of liberal media bias. One has only to do a Net search for 'liberal' 'media bias', to read through many examples relating to current world issues. In the British case you can go to sites such as 'Biased-bbc.blogspot.com'. Books available on key media 'events' include *CNN's Cold War Documentary: Issues and Controversy* (Hoover Press) in which a number of well-known media and academic writers set out a whole raft of criticisms of the factual and liberal travesties in the landmark 'History of the Cold War' CNN/BBC TV co-production. Commissioned by arch-liberal Ted Turner, one should perhaps not be surprised that the production ended up replete with systematic themes of anti-West dogma and a typical pro-liberal agenda. Worst of its sins, however, was its refusal to accept that it was conservative Ronald Reagan's single-minded opposition and plan for communism's defeat that brought the Cold War to an end 'without firing a shot', as Maggie Thatcher so succinctly put it. While the conservative Reagan succeeded in achieving the demise of the 'evil empire' of Soviet communism, the CNN/BBC 'take' ended up by representing Western liberal democracy and communism as morally equivalent. So much then for integrity and good judgment among the CNN/BBC hierarchy responsible for this rare collaborative review of the finest hour of a *conservative* president with a conservative, non-liberal, agenda.

Other excellent books reviewing bias in the media include two by CBS journalist Bernard Goldberg, *Bias: A CBS Insider Exposes How the Media Distorts the News* (Perennial) and *Arrogance: Rescuing America from the*

Media Elite (Warner). Though both concentrate on the US liberal media, many of the issues raised are entirely relevant to the British situation.

New research gets to the heart of the matter

In 2003 research was published into the state of the mass media by the Pew Research Center in the USA. It yielded some fascinating results. In his *US News and World Report* on the findings, John Leo notes, 'What it revealed was that most journalists have political and ideological leanings more liberal than those of the general public'.[8] So confirmatory of what is already perceived as the plain fact of the matter in US circles, Leo suggests a sensible alternative title could easily have been, 'Researchers ferret out the obvious yet again'.

The Pew report found that just 7 per cent of journalists and news executives called themselves 'conservative', compared with 33 per cent of the general American public. As Leo points out, 'The self-identified liberals (34 per cent) are five times as common as conservatives in the news business'. Not surprisingly, when the research was produced it received very little coverage in the media, including the liberal flagship *New York Times*. Quoting liberal Eric Alterman, author of *What Liberal Media?* asking 'why is it such a big deal to have a newsroom that's only a third liberal?', Leo responds that the 'big deal is that media workers are becoming more liberal at a fairly rapid pace — up from 22 per cent nine years ago to 34 per cent now, according to Pew'. Leo adds, 'It would be a bigger deal if the hiring of liberals reached the point (as it has in the academic world) where conservatives don't bother to apply for jobs.' And right there is an insight into why the modern liberal academic world — including the academic Christian world by the way — presently lacks any conservative balance.

Leo goes on to point out that the picture painted by the Pew research actually is more disturbing than it first appears.

For a start, there is an issue over what is meant by 'moderate' or 'mainstream' here. In Leo's experience (and mine) 'liberal journalists tend to think of themselves as representing the mainstream, so in these identification polls, "moderate" usually translates "liberal".' This case is made out further by some of the few social questions posed. As Leo reports, in their answers the 'moderates' actually sounded 'fairly liberal'. When asked whether homosexuality should be approved of by society, 88 per cent of journalists agreed, compared with only 51 per cent of Americans in polls generally. Once again, the imbalance between the much higher percentage of conservative views in the wider population is not reflected among journalists. By way of further confirmation, some 82 per cent of journalists polled were able to list a news agency that was 'especially conservative'. Most (rightly) named the Fox News Channel. But as Leo put it, 'an amazing 62 per cent could not name any news organization that struck them as "especially liberal".' Nearly falling off his chair laughing, Leo comments, 'Good grief. Even 60 per cent of the Homer Simpson family could figure out that the New York Times or National Public Radio qualify as liberal'.[9] To put a British spin on it, most of the *New York Times* editorials make the British leftist *Guardian* newspaper appear almost Thatcherite.

Leo reports that, in their response to the Pew survey, some pointed out that 'personal, social and political views make no difference if a reporter plays the story straight.' 'Yes', says Leo, 'but nearly half of those polled told Pew that journalists too often let their ideological views colour their work.' As Leo says, 'This is a devastating admission, something like an umpire's union reporting that half its membership likes to favour the home team.' He goes on, 'Even apart from loaded reporting, the selection and framing of news stories have a way of reflecting the opinions of editors.'

Leo's article also fixes on a conundrum which has long

perplexed me. It is this: how is it that increasingly liberal newsrooms keep hiring more and more people who do not share the broader conservatism of the general population? In pursuing this question further, Leo hits on a key insight and one with which this writer fully concurs. 'One explanation is that national journalism is now an elite profession, staffed by people who went to elite colleges and who share the conventional views of their class.' The academic community, as Leo indicates, has long been the heartland of liberalism — and it has now managed to influence a generation of budding young journalists to boot. In the Christian community also, theological seminaries and colleges are today largely dominated by liberal academics who gut Christianity of its soul from *inside* the church, succeeding where external liberal forces had failed to affect it for centuries.

Postmodernism has spread through our universities and colleges like a virus inculcating its 'mindset' and values. Somewhat poignantly, I thought, Leo sums it all up with a touching aside.

> When I was at the *New York Times*, the leadership was full of people who had gone to the wrong schools and fought their way up with brains and talent. Two desks away from mine was McCandlish Phillips, a born-again Christian who read the Bible during every break, no matter how brief. Philips was a legendary reporter, rightly treated with awe by the staff, but I doubt he would be hired by most news organizations today. He prayed a lot and had no college degree.[10]

In truth, conservative thinking cannot withstand the 'airbrushing' methods of the modern elitist prospective employer to whom the last thing you would dare impart would be, 'Oh, by the way, I am a practising Christian'. But go in wearing a trendy red HIV/AIDS badge, clutching a copy of Bill Clinton's bulky 'How I did it my conniving way' memoirs and revealing your anti-war, humanitarian credentials, and you are already halfway there. The British and US media love Bill Clinton and hate George Bush. Clinton had sex in the Oval Office and generally brought disgrace to the US presidency. George Bush removed one of the most evil dictators the world has ever seen and freed an entire people from tyranny, and him they hate (at time of writing he is still president). Is there not something despicably amoral about the whole mentality of the Western liberal elite which is able to assume the duality of an arrogant self-esteem in conjunction with such an intellectually and morally perverse perspective? Or is it that it has become so imbued with its own agenda that it can simply no longer discern right from wrong?

So what do we do when the news becomes propaganda? For my own part, I do not share the views of some Americans who would prefer to see their own media adopt a more 'neutral' British style. Some have lately spoken of wanting to remove the openly hostile conservative v. liberal, left v. right, Democrat v. Republican status quo from the media battlefield. But, while the US style of presenting and sometimes commenting on the news is something of a shock for the British viewer initially, it does have the double boon of honesty and transparency. In the USA, quite often, gone is the shallow pretence of 'impartiality'. In Britain, however, one is led to believe that the 'mainstream' is representative of no specific political or philosophical perspective. Regular assessment on the other hand, reveals plainly that what one is hearing is slanted relentlessly 'left of centre'. For all its faults and frailties — and the same thing applies to the freedom of speech that Americans presently enjoy in their media, but which has long since disappeared in the British broadcast media — I much prefer the American system. At least we can be in little doubt as to the 'slant' of a particular broadcaster, journalist or channel.

Fox News has an excellent example of how this can work well. One of Fox's best programmes is presented by Sean Hannity (a vocal conservative) and Alan Colmes (a vocal liberal). Together they interview conservatives and liberals alike and both throw in comments along the way. Quite often the sparks do fly. But — and this is the important thing — *all* is properly debated out in the open, leaving the viewer/listener to make up their own mind. Whether we prefer this approach or not, it has the benefit of regularly getting straight to the heart of the matter — and doing so without the paralysing fear of controversy.[11] In my view, the result is that the observer's understanding is often greatly enhanced — and often in a way *not* intended by the 'vocal' presenter/interviewee, right or left.

The fact is that every one of us approaches each situation, including the latest news report, with a particular worldview. Whether we are consumers, reporters, editors or presenters of news, it would be terribly helpful if we both recognized that, more often than not, there is an angle to how news is presented, and we just want everyone participating in the process to be honest about it. But the critical issue for me, however, is that the liberal mindset, *more* than the conservative one, is either reluctant to do so, or is in denial that what it professes as 'mainstream' views are in fact not mainstream at all, but rather its own liberal views.

The trouble is that liberal news reporting, in the guise of being 'mainstream', is today dominating our supposedly 'balanced' media. This means that the predominantly conservative views of the general population, including those who hold a theistic worldview, are being ignored, despised and constantly refuted by subtle and pervasive liberal propaganda. It is also propaganda that reflects neither the views nor the values of its consumers. And like the first casualty of war, the first casualty of a liberal-dominated media will be truth. As a fine journalist like McCandlish Phillips would have no doubt agreed:

> *These are the things you should do. Speak each man the truth to his neighbour;*
> *Give judgment in your gates for truth, justice and peace* (Zechariah 8:16).

---

[1] See the details in my opening essay 'Saddam, The Death Penalty and Other Moral Issues of the Day' in this volume.

[2] The Centre for Policy Studies recently produced a report which cited 'overwhelming' bias by the BBC in favour of pro-European opinion. The CPS studies based their findings on an analysis of the way the BBC reported the Government's announcement in the summer of 2004 that it would hold a referendum on the proposed European Constitution. The CPS studied 28 separate reports on BBC1, BBC2 and BBC Radio 4 where Europhiles took up 61 per cent of interview time, with Eurosceptics getting just under 30 per cent.

[3] The media continually assumes the homosexual population to be in the region of ten per cent. The actual statistics, however, point to a much smaller 1.6 per cent of the population claiming to be practising homosexuals.

[4] As we saw in part 2 of the essay 'War and Peace', also in this volume.

[5] ibid.

[6] See the article 'Who killed David Kelly?', also in this volume.

[7] Report 'BBC credibility "on line" over shoddy journalism standards' by Chris Hastings in the Daily Telegraph, 4 July 2004. The shoddy journalism was mostly geared to reports by local BBC regions and its online service — which happens to be the most popular news website in Europe, receiving 1.9 billion hits a month!

[8] John Leo, 'Liberal Media? I'm Shocked!', US News and World Report online archive, 7 June, 2004.

[9] For those not 'in the know', the *New York Times* is regularly cited in

the US media as 'flagship of the left'.

10 John Leo, 'Liberal Media? I'm Shocked!', US News and World Report online archive, June 7, 2004.

11 It is the inherent fear of controversy and giving offence, with the British propensity always to seek compromise (*not* a virtue when the issue is truth), which, in my view, lies at the heart of the malaise in modern British culture and life.

ISSUES: the battle for the mind
(& the right to defend one's home)

6
Liberal and conservative thinking[1]
A political mindset or a whole way of reasoning?

In a stopover in Atlanta, en route to London, I picked up a copy of Ann Coulter's explosive bestseller *Scandal: Liberal Lies About the American Right*,[2] a polemic against private agendas and the inherent bias of the liberal-dominated media in the USA. With my background in freelance journalism, Coulter's own lawyer status (I was a paralegal in a former life, too), and her flair for powerfully worded logic (an increasingly lost art in the UK in public and media circles), I was engaged by her presentation of a mass of evidence revealing the perversity of liberal thinking among the American political and media elites. A way of thinking on key issues which — if a whole raft of Gallup and other polls are to be believed — is not at all reflective of the far more conservatively-minded population of the USA.

I have a growing interest in American politics generally, especially since 9/11. But what Coulter's book confirmed for me was yet another strong melding of US-UK cultural convergence: a powerful propensity toward liberal-dominated thinking on just about any serious moral and political issue, with a strong and consistent theme of anti-Christian bigotry — which some US commentators have already dubbed 'Christophobia' — thrown in for good measure. No wonder in the UK that the Prime Minister's former press secretary, Alistair Campbell, was moved to inform the Labour Government's inner sanctum, 'we don't do God'. God no longer sits well, or is good politics, in the progressively Godless society, at least as far as liberal elitism is concerned.

But one other aspect of Coulter's book which set me thinking (although she did not allude to it all) was the strong parallel between the nature of liberal thinking in the world of politics and the media, and the increasingly liberalized thinking of almost all sections of the modern (largely irrelevant) church leadership. But let me not run ahead of myself. The parallel between the USA and the UK in terms of a growing pro-liberal bias in politics and the media in British public life was nowhere more forcefully brought into perspective recently than in the collusion between the BBC and a Member of Parliament in backtracking on their commitment to allow 'the people' a shot at playing a direct role in exercising their democratic rights. And in their shabby treatment of the voting public, both the parliamentarians involved and the BBC revealed their true colours and their pompous liberal agendas, which would not for one moment countenance that the 'conservative' people might know better than they — with their growing sense of impotence at the modern liberal carve-up in politics, which is increasingly not working for them or for the greater good of society.

During 2003, Labour MP Stephen Pound came up with a spiffing broadcasting wheeze which was duly taken up by BBC Radio 4's *Today* morning news programme over the Christmas and New Year period. It afforded listeners the unique opportunity to put forward a 'listener's law' which Mr Pound would sponsor and attempt to steer through Parliament onto the statute books. No doubt Pound's personal intention was to present himself as a 'champion of the people'. In the event he turned out to be anything but that, and exposed his own deep-seated ambivalence to true democracy into the bargain.

No doubt the BBC hierarchy, believing the myth (as it turned out) that its listeners were predominantly card-carrying latitudinarians, had thought that proposals would revolve around issues such as dogs fouling the footpaths, or some other 'jolly' and largely insignificant area of law. Both they and Pound, however, were in for a real shock. For all the humour that attended the broadcasting exercise, it was at root a genuine opportunity (or so it seemed when the *Today* programme originally sold its listeners the idea) for voters who were increasingly feeling disenfranchised from the system that passes for democracy in the UK, for once to have a real say. I have no doubt that, had the BBC asked Ann Coulter what might result from such an offer, she could have warned them exactly what might well happen next. And what did happen next gave us a real insight into the chasm which has developed between the concerns of a conservatively-minded, practical people and the speculations of a liberally-minded, intellectually theoretical, liberal political and media elite. The issue which exposed it all was the very basic right of the citizen to defend his family and his property in his home.

An exercise in true democracy

In 1999, the UK public had engaged in a genuine debate over the case of Norfolk farmer Tony Martin. Martin, having been burgled for the umpteenth time in his rural Norfolk farmhouse (about which police had been able to do precisely nothing in terms of protecting him), finally snapped. In the dead of night he shot two burglars, killing one of them by using an illegally-held pump-action shotgun. But when Martin was subsequently charged with criminal offences and duly brought to trial, ultimately being convicted of manslaughter, the general public were incensed at the prospect that the law itself had effectively made Martin and not the burglars the real criminal, yet all he was doing was protecting himself against two (for all he knew, armed) criminals. The public watched with a sense of growing horror as Martin was not only given five years' imprisonment, but was later refused early parole because of his 'lack of remorse'. But why, pray, should Martin show remorse? He was eventually released having served two-thirds of his sentence.

What incensed the predominantly conservatively-thinking general public over this appalling treatment were two things: first, criminal recidivists, merely by 'expressing remorse' (whether they mean it or not), are released back onto the streets in double-quick time; and second, the system was revealing itself to be, in practice if not in theory, more concerned for the rights of the criminal than for the rights of the victim. Something was badly amiss here, and the average citizen knew it, even if the judiciary, Parliament and the BBC did not.

So when the *Today* programme producers decided to go ahead with Mr Pound's 'silly-season' gambit offering listeners the opportunity to put forward their favoured new piece of legislation, it was the Martin case and the need to reform the law that affected these situations which surfaced above all else. And Pound and the BBC were about to receive a hard lesson in reality[3]; in which they, as liberal intellectuals, having assumed the public mood to be (or rather should be) the same as theirs, find out that it is they who are in the real minority. Increasingly upset by the propensity of a disengaged, often activist, judiciary too ready to reveal a disproportionate concern for individual human rights above communal ones, the 'listening public' duly exacted its revenge. To the horror of BBC executives and of Pound, the public chose five laws they would like to see enacted; plumping ultimately, by some margin, for a new law allowing 'homeowners to defend their home from intruders *by any means*'.

The whole affair had now gone far enough, however, and the poll sponsors colluded to scotch the 'fun': revealing, as all upset liberals do, their despising of the 'ignorant masses', and their supercilious 'knowing better' arrogance which rises to the surface whenever their personal agenda has been ruffled. Now squirming with obvious embarrassment and assuming their best anti-democratic, pompous and traditional 'your listeners don't really understand' mode, Pound and the BBC backed away from the whole concept of sponsoring the law, or indeed any law — especially the one the public actually wanted. And let us not forget for one moment that these 'pillars of society', the BBC, sitting MPs, the array of liberal pundits like Simon Jenkins of *The Times,* and even the Deputy Prime Minister, all 'tut-tutting' in their own 'told you so' liberal-know-it-all fashion, perceive themselves to be true upholders of the democratic tradition. In truth, however — as Coulter and various non-liberals (including me) will tell you — liberals may, as they do in America, formally call themselves Democrats, but liberals everywhere are *anything but* true democrats when 'push comes to shove', because their true politics, indeed faith, is their own privatised, liberalizing, *minority* agenda. So much then for *true* democracy being alive and well in the land of the Mother of Parliaments.

An exercise in true democracy: epilogue
Now I should say that as a 'conservative thinker', I fully recognize (as no doubt did most of the voters in the BBC poll) that there would need to be some caveats to such a law.

But what I and they (according to the vast majority of responses when Pound and the BBC backed away from their commitment) did not expect, is that the whole matter would be dropped so spectacularly, reflecting (and bearing out the growing public concern) that the Government, the judiciary and the nation's public broadcaster had no intention of pursuing the public's general concern over their perceived disenfranchisement, and specifically over this important 'defending one's home' issue.

What was implicit throughout this whole affair is the general public's deep concern over the nature of the present law and its interpretation, especially in the boundaries of what constitutes a use of (the absurdly inadequately worded) 'proportionate force'. No one wants to see a 'shoot on sight' law introduced. We do not want unidentified visitors — even hawkers! — shot on sight as they enter through our gates. And what if someone should take a wrong turn and enter the unlocked door of our flat or apartment by genuine mistake? Certainly caveats need to be written in. But as the law stands, not least in the way it is being practically administered, the homeowner currently must live as much in fear of the retribution of the law, as from invasive night-callers. The plain emphasis and onus of the law has shifted from where it might once have been, to the detriment of the average good citizen. The public plea, throughout the Tony Martin case and, as revealed in the BBC poll, is thus to shift the onus back where it belongs, and where morality (and God's law specifically) demands that it should be. In that way the prospective felon will know exactly where he/she stands, should they be minded to infringe the most basic right of protection in the home, making the whole area (socially and morally) irrevocably sacrosanct.

In the ensuing debate, the underlying nature of anti-democratic liberal thinking surfaced more overtly — especially in the erroneous assessment that giving the populist masses direct democratic access in this way is, implicitly, 'not a good idea'. Indeed, this denial of true democracy is implicitly written into the American Electoral College system, whose founders themselves did not consider the 'ignorant masses' worthy to possess direct access to the levers of power, and so saw to it that they did not have it.

Revealing the extent of his embarrassment at the outcome of the BBC poll, Stephen Pound wryly attempted to play down the furore by quoting Mark Twain's insightful remark, 'The people have spoken — the bastards'. And now the liberal elite came out in force both to denigrate Pound and the BBC for their naivety, and, unwittingly, to reveal their general lack of integrity, as much as their lack of faith in true democracy. By denying the 'voice of the people' in this key public issue, by dropping the whole notion of pursuing public concerns *entirely*, what the 'we know better' advocates did was to condemn all of us (including them — are liberal homes any more safe?) to live in fear not only of domestic break-ins, but also the uncertainty of what we can do about it in practice, and especially the more vulnerable among us.

Simon Jenkins of *The Times*, noting Pound's severe embarrassment, asserted, 'He might have hoped to become a hero of the airwaves by championing a bill to save rhinos or uphold motherhood. Instead he must now sponsor legislation for what he predicts would be the mass slaughter of 16-year olds with pump-action shotguns. That is what happens, Mr Pound, when you sell your soul to the media.' The straightforward implication of the observation is that Mr Jenkins scolds Pound for 'selling one's soul to the media' and, implicitly, for having the naivety to allow the public a free vote in the first place. Jenkins comment might even be understood as carrying some force and integrity had he not earlier asserted about the same poll: 'The show reminds me of the old *Daily Mirror* at its best. There is virtue in a listeners' law after all...I am sure that the BBC would declare this as no more than their original intention. A listeners' law is better than no law at all. Where indeed would we be without the BBC?' Mr Jenkins, like many others of his ilk, has no compunction in doing a *volte-face* whenever the going gets tough in the logic stakes, in order not to offend his liberalizing ideals. The Deputy Prime Minister, in his own inimitable 'knockabout' style and equally non-democratic way, waded in thus: 'I'm afraid that's the kind of vigilante law that I don't think Parliament would agree to'. That's funny. I thought Parliament (including Mr Prescott and Mr Pound) was elected to 'represent' and 'serve the interests of' the people, not merely themselves and their own minority agenda? My mistake.

But it is in the 'asides', the secondary comments on this whole sordid affair, that we discern the underlying 'anti'-intellectual biases at work in their complexity and perversity. Mr Pound told the *Independent* newspaper, 'we are going to have to re-evaluate the listenership of Radio 4. I would have expected this result if there had been a poll in *The Sun*'. It seems then that liberal thinkers are unable to see that no matter what our 'listening' or 'reading preferences' are, there are some issues which are so much at the heart of social life that the public is actually agreed upon them by reason of its socially 'conservative' nature. Rather, for the elite, it must mean 're-assessing' the profile of listenerships/readerships in terms of their own liberalizing ideals (in other words, be careful to control the democratic process according to one's own ideals). This is because liberals are such a vocal minority that they even perceive themselves as holding majority views, which they patently do not.

It was the *Daily Mail*'s Leo McKinstry who perhaps got closest to putting his finger on the pulse of the nation's (that of Radio 4 listeners and *Sun* readers combined) conservative feeling on this issue, observing, 'For all its humour, the

Today poll graphically highlights the mounting frustration of the British public, of all classes and races, with the way this country is being governed...If the *Today* programme brings that mood to the notice of our political leaders, it will have performed a far better service than could be achieved through all its other worthy features'. Even that most overt of liberal agenda newspapers, *The Guardian*, through Nicholas Watt, reported, 'Nearly 10,000 listeners had confounded critics of the [Today] programme, often dismissed as the liberal elite's talking shop, to vote for a measure championed by the Tory right'.

But, in all of this, what we may perceive perhaps, above all else, is that the liberal mindset just doesn't 'get it' at all. It can't quite see why the majority of right-thinking citizens perceive that it is far more important to protect the homeowner's rights,and not regard them *as equal to* the rights of the evil-intentioned, possibly murderous, night callers. They cannot quite see why it is so ridiculous to speak of the use of 'proportionate force' in the home, when that homeowner is an enfeebled senior citizen; a sick person; a single woman; a child; an ageing, remote, farmer living in constant fear; or any one of us. Was Martin, are any of us, seriously expected to tussle with burly interlopers in the early hours of the morning, not knowing whether they are armed and whether, if they overcome us, they will go on to murder or rape our wives or hurt our children? What absurdity of the modern legal system insists that we restrict ourselves in some theoretical way to show only 'proportionate force'? Like many members of the concerned, conservative-minded public, I would have no compunction at all — given that the circumstances of the illegal entry into the home, especially at the dead of night, are plain enough — with allowing any homeowner the right to 'brain' the interloper with a baseball bat or any other heavy object that will do the job; or even, if necessary, shooting an intruder with a legally owned weapon.

More important than my view, however, is that God himself does not view this as murder or criminal or even immoral. In a passage dealing *specifically* with this issue of the right of persons to defend their home, the writer of the Book of Exodus gives us God's plain teaching (which in turn reveals the growing Godlessness being practised by the contemporary liberal-dominated judiciary) when he says:

> If the thief is found breaking in, and he is struck so that he dies, *there shall be no guilt for his bloodshed.* (Exodus 22:2)

Just what part of this God-given understanding does the liberal mind find difficult to understand? There is so much at stake when an illegal intruder enters the home, that God gives his creatures the right, if necessary, to strike the intruder without suffering 'bloodguilt'.

If we continue to administer the law in the way that we currently are, increasingly endangering the family and the home, the most basic building block of all societies, then we can not only expect the public to lose confidence in the rule of law, but also bring upon ourselves, still further, the wrath of God, who will not stomach our indifference and disobedience for long. The deep-felt public concern over the gross injustice suffered by Tony Martin (albeit he had used an illegally-held firearm) is a genuine reflection of society's increasing disquiet with growing liberal, anti-common good biases which are steadily eroding public confidence in the laws by which we are all governed.

What is also worthy of note, however, is the disturbing reality of the hidden agenda of the modern liberal: on the face of it, democratic, free and open; beneath the surface, antidemocratic where liberal values are at stake; tied to a rigid individualizing perspective on life; but, perhaps worst of all, hardly ever up-front about where they are truly coming from. Conservative thinkers may not be without their faults, but one that will not normally be numbered among them is having a hidden agenda. Unlike liberals, conservatives at least can often be counted upon to be marked by transparency in both thought and deed. Once we get a handle on all of this, we begin to see how such thinking has today become endemic among populist politicians, the activist judiciary, the elite academia and the modern environmental terrorists and, sadly, the mainstream leadership of the modern church.

The battle for the mind in an increasingly liberal church
Whether it is in the USA or the UK, whether the issue is a key political one or not, it seems that the debate between the conservative and liberal is not really about thinking politically, rather is it about thinking *per se*. And the same is certainly true in the modern church. Indeed, reading through Coulter's book, it was hard not to see a powerful affinity between the nature of conservative and liberal thinking in the world and that which is progressively pervading the modern church leader, including the formerly conservative, but lately liberal, neo-evangelical church leadership.

In the evangelical world, the issue of moral, biblically informed thinking was regularly the concern of the late Francis Schaeffer. It is also a matter raised by Christian thinkers and cultural commentators such as Os Guinness in his *Fit Minds, Fat Bodies: Why evangelicals don't think and what to do about it*, and Professor Mark Noll's *The Scandal of the Evangelical Mind*. The world is already used to watching the modern church's shameful practice of moving paedophile bishops and immoral vicars and pastors between livings, to protect them from the due process of civil (and *God-ordained*, see Rom. 13:1; 1 Peter 2:13-14) authority; when the church should be sacking them as men unfit for office and, on occasions, turning them over to the civil authorities. Here is the liberal mindset in amoral, even immoral, ecclesiastic action: once again marked by the perception that the individual rights of the miscreant are more important that the more pressing health of the whole community. And neither is such thinking confined to issues of sexuality in parts of the blatantly non-Bible-believing, Roman Catholic or Protestant liberal church.

In an increasingly fractured and separatist, modern evangelicalism, false teachers of all kinds, who hold little accord with the teaching of historic Christianity, are today flourishing visibly, unopposed. In the contemporary Christian 'marketplace', tolerance has become, through the influence of both modern and postmodern mindsets, the chief of virtues. But what is new in the church is that tolerance has come to mean tolerance towards all manner of false teaching; where the bestselling book lists and the religious media are dominated by some of the most unedifying, non-biblical beliefs; where leading theologians practise 'academic' faith, denying key aspects of God's attributes, such as his foreknowledge and control over the future[4]; and where, perversely, leading agencies of the church, such as the National Association of Evangelicals in America and the Evangelical Alliance in the UK, *refuse* to call this heresy or error, much less eject those responsible for it.

The more conservative-minded, church-reputation-caring Christian is aghast at what the modern liberal church leader will allow next. Even more disturbing is how those who consider themselves 'conservative', and not 'liberal' at all, are colluding with liberal thinking by adopting shameful silences for the sake of avoiding public controversy. It is achieved easily by merely adopting a strategy of keeping heads in the theological sand, and hoping against hope that these guys and their teaching might just go away. The trouble is that liberal seeds sink their roots into the soil if they are not vigorously pulled out. And they grow, choking the tilled ground with human philosophy and not the conservative Bible teaching of the 'old faith'. For just like the liberal in the world, the liberal in the church may be different *by degree* (being often conservative in theory, while liberal in practice), but *not* different *in kind*.

This is precisely why the conservative-minded apostle Paul was so angry with the timid, liberal-minded Galatians (Gal. 1) and Corinthians (1 Cor 5; 2 Cor. 11) who were prepared to allow individuals to pervert the thinking of the whole community. Contrary to the spirit of the modern leader who practises a *laissez-faire* pragmatic 'theology' and amorality, Paul's response to immorality, amorality, heresy and error was quite different. Such was his concern for the common good above the individual's good that he exposed any diversion from the right path. Even the apostle Peter came in for a tongue-lashing from Paul when he (Gal. 2:11), by his actions, was considered to be threatening the greater good of the community.

The evangelical church, as with the church generally, has undoubtedly lapsed into a period of chronic 'niceness' concerning the stomaching of false teaching in the church — a fact the world observes. Yet Paul warns us against fellowshipping with those who 'cause division and offences, contrary to doctrine' (Rom. 16:17) and not to 'keep company with anyone *named a brother* who is a fornicator, or covetous, or an idolator', etc. (1 Cor. 5:11, italics mine — a teaching which applies *only* to those who publicly call themselves Christians, and not unbelievers). And slap bang in the middle of a list of the more familiar felonies which disbar some from heaven altogether (Gal. 5:20), we find that 'selfish ambition, dissensions and heresies' are included. What are 'dissensions' but liberal, independent-mindedness which demurs from the orthodox historic teaching of the church? In confronting heresy we may not judge the final state of the heretic (for they may yet repent), but we are *specifically* called to judge their present teaching. And in doing so we will be acting as biblical and conservative thinkers, those whose greater concern is for the reputation of Christ's body, the church in the world, above the individual.

Coulter says of liberals in the world: 'Prevarication and denigration are the hallmarks of liberal argument. Logic is not their metier'.[5] Neither is it the metier of liberals in the church. Liberals do not like logical debate and especially, therefore, logical Calvinist-style biblical theology. Indeed, they rarely engage with conservatives in any meaningful way at all, preferring to respond with anger (at the notion of absolute truth) in a postmodern world and church. Or they settle simply for *ad hominen* attacks and name-calling, like liberals through the ages. Where conservative thinkers welcome thoughtful argument, liberals invoke pietistic arrogance. In a similar vein neo-evangelicals today tag their beliefs with private, non-catholic, Scripture-twisting.[6]

It has often been said that liberals are the most 'illiberal of people'. I have found this to be true. They refuse to align themselves with the confessional mind of the historic church community (implicitly denying it, and effectively history, a voice at all). Yet the Protestant Reformers were fond of reiterating that they agreed with the church fathers in their understanding of the catholic oneness of the church, and with its teaching of that *form* of apostolic doctrine delivered to it, making it a truly confessional church.

On a moral level, only a liberal mindset could attempt to hold in tension the absurd juxtaposition that abortion is right while the death penalty for murderers is wrong — that *the guilty* should live, while *the innocent* should die. What perverse thinking established such absurdly immoral beliefs at the heart of the church? Even if we should give the liberal-mind 'more rope' (if you will forgive the pun) and allow that the death penalty may be a crime against an individual life, there is no leeway to construe it as a crime against the community. Yet is not abortion a crime against God first — and against the whole community second?

Conclusion

Coulter depicts liberals in the world as being 'painfully self-righteous, with fantastic hatreds', who 'could not see the other fellow's position if you prodded them with white-hot pokers'.[7] When it comes to the thinking of Christian liberals, in their more overt ecumenical Roman Catholic and broad Protestant forms, or in their more insidious neo-evangelical guises, it is painfully pietistic, self-righteous, and tolerant of all manner of error — and those responsible for that error. In fact, their only real irritant, the one who really gets under their skin (just as for the worldly liberal), is the conservative thinker — the Christian who actually believes what God has said through his Word, and seeks to pursue and apply it in practice, both personally and (openly) in society.

True faith and a true social conscience will always reveal themselves as being concerned, above all else, with catholicity of living faith and concern for the community as a whole. For conservative Christians, the concept of going against God's will on any issue is merely to play King Canute.[8] If then we claim to be Christians, whether we perceive ourselves currently as conservative or liberal thinkers, we should know that thinking *biblically* — being renewed in the spirit of our minds — is what God himself wants of us; that we will yet become model church members *as well as* model good citizens. But to think as liberals is consistently to run the risk of not only falling foul of God's laws, but of the laws of logic, too.

---

[1] These terms should not be thought to be coterminous with the names of current political parties. For a start present-day political party thinking is often inconsistent with the parties' own founding principles.

[2] Ann Coulter, *Scandal: Liberal Lies About the American Right* (New York: Three Rivers Press, 2002).

[3] Anyone who thinks for one moment that the UK has a truly democratic system really does need to get out and about more.

[4] Open Theists deny that God knows the future in any detail.

[5] Coulter, op. cit., p. 2.

[6] Such as the widespread use by false teachers of the Matthew 18:15 'defence' — that which in context applies only to moral issues in local fellowship situations and has nothing to say to issues affecting public teaching of church doctrine.

[7] Coulter, op. cit., p. 33.

[8] In fact, this is somewhat unfair. Canute was no fool. What he was actually doing in his seaside jaunt was showing his subjects that even kings possess *no* divine ability to hold back the tide (rather than the common, misguided assertion that that was what he was actually attempting to do).

ISSUES: identifying personal patterns of belief

7
So What *Is* Your Worldview?
*Because you **do** have one*

Every one of us has a worldview, a view by which we perceive the world and how we think, speak and act upon that perception. Whether we are aware of it or not, have ever given it much thought, or are able to articulate it, we shall find, if we give it but a few moments thought, that we *do* have one. Perhaps the best and most marvellously succinct way of explaining it comes from one commentator who describes a worldview as 'a coherent frame of reference for all thought and action'.[1]

Even those who perceive themselves as the most 1960s retro-hippy, anarchistic, freedom loving liberals, hold an identifiable worldview. For a start, anarchists and liberals, who consider themselves tolerant of all views and free of all dogma, are among the most *intolerant* and *dogmatic* of people. It has frequently been said that 'liberals are often the most illiberal of people'. This is because the 'dogma-less' anarchist's very starting point is an illusion. Anarchists relish their liberal credentials. They see themselves as 'freer' than others. But they are just as locked into a pattern of identifiable dogmatic beliefs as anyone else. Being thoroughly postmodern people[2], they believe themselves to be the most tolerant of individuals, believing in the moral equivalence of *all* belief systems — *except*, that is, those held by conservatives[3] upon whom they will often unload the most intolerant of verbiage, wholly blind to the irony of their own, very real, intolerance.

They reject all religious faiths, describing them as 'psychological crutches', yet failing to grasp that they themselves 'lean' just as heavily on their own psychological system of belief. They are committed to individualism, the spirit of our age. They are beholden to none, seeing themselves as citizens of the world rather than any country. Neither do they believe that their liberal freedoms and rights as individuals in any way conflict with the wider freedoms and rights of the community. They fail entirely to acknowledge that 'one man's freedom is often another man's burden'.[4] The 'anarchist' here is of course being caricatured for the sake of argument. But it is a perfectly valid 'extreme' example which reveals that anarchists too have worldviews governing both their beliefs and their actions.

It may be that we just don't care what our worldview, or the worldview of others, is. And that's fine. But, if we have any regard at all for truth and reason in life, then understanding our worldview, and that of others, can tell us much about our own capacity to be logical and reasoned; why we speak and act as we do. For the truth is that in life we *do* as we believe. Our opinions, views, beliefs and actions are thus all underpinned by our worldview — an identifiable pattern of belief that governs our whole life. When we start to draw together the loose and disparate strands of our personal beliefs, what they add up to can be a very interesting 'whole'.

So what is my worldview?
James W. Sire, in his excellent book *The Universe Next Door: A Basic Worldview Catalog*, in a longer definition

than that already stated, says a worldview is 'a set of presuppositions (assumptions which may be true, partially true, or entirely false) which we hold (consciously or subconsciously, consistently or inconsistently) about the basic make-up of our world.'[5]

For the sake of clarity, as is made plain from the rest of this book, my worldview is theistic or biblical. That is, I believe in a Creator God who made all things, and that knowledge of the Creator God can be gained, not by mystical means, but, primarily, through the pages of the Bible, the written and eternal revelation of God to mankind. Through this I am aware of the atoning sacrifice of Jesus Christ, God the Son, on the Cross, and that he takes away my sins and the sins of the whole world through faith in him. All my relationships, my views, and my life are thus governed chiefly by what the Bible has to teach me about those things. My morality is what I would call the 'gold standard' by which *all* moralities can be measured, the Ten Commandments. Sunday is *the* day (the Lord's Day) for worshipping the living God in community. And in this I am not just stating my preferences or beliefs, but expounding what the Bible and the historic church have always taught plainly on these matters — even though liberal Christians do their best to water them down.

As we shall see later, by no means all modern churchgoers or Christians hold a biblical or (amazingly) even a theistic worldview. This, however, does not negate the fact that there is such a thing as a Christian theistic or biblical worldview, and that, for two thousand years, this had been the prevailing worldview. In our age however, it may be said that the prevailing worldview is no longer one that believes in a Creator God and absolute truth, but one which believes all truth to be subjective and relative in a universe which came about by accident and not design (at least not the design of any god) — in other words a postmodern worldview.

The Politics of Faith

My reason for setting out all this here is twofold. First, to make plain where I am coming from, and second, to extend the invitation for you, dear reader, to do the same for yourself — and perhaps with others — for this reason: that each of us may be able to both define our belief system and defend it with integrity for more than two minutes! You see, the reality is this: most people are simply (not having defined it) intellectually unable to defend their worldview. They much prefer to disparage the often more cogent and considered worldviews of others, leaving their own belief system as 'undefined', thus absolving themselves from receiving the same treatment they and others are prepared to mete out to anyone with the temerity to disagree with them.

The problem I have with some who do not profess the Christian faith is that they are quite prepared to attack a biblical worldview (or indeed any worldview) while not seeing themselves 'accountable' for their own particular beliefs in exactly the same way. As a long-time Christian I am perfectly able to set forth my spectrum or pattern of biblical beliefs in a cohesive whole. Whether I am right or wrong to hold those beliefs is not the point. The fact is that I can provide an apologia for them that is both reasonable and logical and indeed has the added dimension of historical longevity going for it (not that some would give that much weight). Mine would be the same pattern of confessional conformity as was held by the church fathers (a linear line of great church leaders), as set forth in the great ecumenical confessions of the church right through from the early creeds and the Reformed medieval confessions of faith. They are far from mine alone. It is essentially the same biblical worldview as held by the apostolic founders of the New Testament church, through Augustine to Luther, Calvin, Spurgeon and so on. My point is this: it is a worldview with which I am fully able to spend days, if not weeks, boring the reader to death! Why? Because it so governs my life and is so readily identifiable as a coherent system of articulated belief, that I am able to express the holistic logic of it. If the Protestant Reformation had different strands of emphasis to it, nowhere were those strands better drawn together than in the Calvinistic (after the great French theologian John Calvin) scheme of things, as far as I am concerned. Indeed, it was in (what for me had become) the full-orbed, reasoned and marvellous logic of the Reformed faith that I began to marvel at the 'hand of God' behind it all. Now I do not propose to distress the reader here by articulating why I believe that the biblical (and especially Reformed) worldview bears on every area of life, as no other pattern of belief does. No doubt there are others out there who might wax as lyrical about their own worldview — and for an equal amount of time! But the reality is that, though most hold a postmodern worldview, not all can string together even a handful of intellectual reasons why. In other words, their beliefs are not intellectually apprehended, nor are they scientifically defended: they are simply held *by faith*. And not only by faith but, unlike my own for which I can give very reasoned arguments, by blind faith at that!

In truth, they are exhibiting far more faith in their understanding of the world than do I. Yet these same individuals (and it is the majority in society), who hold to humanist, evolutionary, New Age beliefs and count all these as equally valid (postmodernism), are often unable to give cogent reasons for their beliefs or worldview beyond a couple of bald assertions over a two-minute period.

But if we were to ask the average person, say family or friends, just two or three simple questions concerning their beliefs about life, it would be perfectly possible to draw together their strands of belief into a recognizable holistic worldview.[6] Once done, a number of things quickly become *very* apparent. First, when confronted by their own, now articulated, pattern of belief, many are often surprised that,

The Politics of Faith

just like *any* religious believer, much of it is held by faith alone. Second, it is often a pattern of belief lacking any real logic, indeed a system which holds opposing realities in tension. Third, many individuals have no idea where these beliefs come from and can provide not the slightest defence for holding them. And yet, the very *same* individuals will probably demand (often aggressively) that a religious believer be able to defend their faith throughout a most intensive and systematic grilling. This is precisely why I mentioned above that I could articulate my own faith and worldview for days. The reality is, however, that it is often the case that someone who holds an 'evolutionary worldview',[7] cannot even support or defend their theory with even the merest scrap of supportive argument, reason and logic for a few minutes, let alone a few hours! That is because most evolutionary 'theorists' also have a 'religious' faith. But while they demand that the religious believer, especially a Christian theist like myself, should 'prove' and articulate his, they see no valid reason why they should be called upon to 'prove' and defend theirs.

I am quite prepared to take my chances in the marketplace of ideas with my Christian beliefs, just so long as we have a level playing field. Religious and philosophical tolerance is a mainstay of my belief system. I do not wish ever to force my beliefs on someone else. I am however only too pleased to 'give a reason for the hope that is in me' as God, through the apostle Peter, requires. That will not mean meekly accepting all other systems as equally true and valid when it comes to discussion and debate. But neither does it mean that disagreement will turn into violent confrontation. You don't have to agree with someone to love them. The problem is that some faith systems are so intolerant that they are too bigoted to allow such genuine freedom to others! And this is where, by articulating our worldviews, each one of us, for the first time, can create a level playing field for genuine discussion and debate — seeing *all* systems and worldviews as, ultimately, faith-based. Only then can we examine the claims of each in turn, both in its detailed parts (its tenets of faith) and its holistic pattern (its worldview). And one of the best, and perhaps most comfortable, ways to enter into this arena in a non-threatening environment, is when we socialize together.

Playing the 'After-Dinner Chat Game'
It is not my intention here to set forth the pros and cons of the various worldviews, nor to discuss the merits or otherwise of each. This has been done admirably elsewhere and I would encourage the reader further on this whole issue. One could do a lot worse than obtain a copy of James Sire's excellent book, which has seen over one million copies printed, mainly for use in universities (see footnote 1 for details). Sire and others highlight what are the major patterns of thinking which make up our many worldviews.

Among the worldviews, he identifies the theistic (the belief that God made the world and all creatures in it for a purpose); the deist naturalist (the belief that God made the world but then left it to run its 'natural' course); the nihilist (the denial of the possibility of any real knowledge); the existentialist (in its atheistic form that: God does not exist. The cosmos exists as a uniformity of cause and effect in a 'closed system'. In its theistic form that: it focuses attention on human nature and subjective spiritual experience above objective biblical truth); the eastern pantheist (God is the cosmos, God is all that exists, everything is God); New Age or eastern mysticism (there is no God or all is God and life is a mystical experience), and postmodern (truth is relative, truth is whatever is true for you). Neither is it my purpose here to identify any particular worldview, though postmodernism is likely to feature most in liberal Western thinking and society. Before we proceed further, let me say this. The object of the exercise is not to lose ourselves in technical detail by attempting to 'pigeonhole' ourselves and everyone else with whom we make contact under one or other of these and other worldviews. My purpose here is much more basic. It is rather to put to ourselves and to others just a few basic questions to begin the process toward establishing and understanding that we all have a worldview, that it is essentially faith-based, and that we act according to that worldview — and to get ourselves and others thinking to that end. The bottom line is this: whether we hold a theistic worldview, or any of the variety of non-theistic ones, each one of us can have little to say about that held by another, if we cannot articulate an understanding of our own.

Where theistic worldviews have been set out and stated for centuries (this is no discussion about relative religions, but about relative worldviews[8]) they are readily identifiable. But while many today, perhaps for the first time in history, hold to a non-theistic position, their worldviews are often not intellectually apprehended. The very mark of modern man is often gross ignorance about all the big questions in life: including the greatest of all: why? We may disagree with the confessional status of various religions (and I do), but they at least have the basic merit of putting forth a construction which most of us may find easy to disparage, while failing to see the essential illogical idiocy of our own scheme of things! And if you are a Christian reading this, may I suggest that next time you are relentlessly pursued (as is the wont of the modern cynic), turn the conversation around and put the beliefs of your pursuer on the spot instead. It is not a question of whether he or she has faith or not: the real question is 'in what', 'in whom' or 'where' is their particular faith. If you have taken the trouble to examine your own worldview and know its component parts, then the least you can expect when others want to shoot down yours is that they can make themselves vulnerable to the same verbal treatment. The 'default position' for far too many cynics today, however, is to attack the beliefs of others in ignorance that their own house is often 'built on sand'. It is perhaps high time they were faced with this fact.

If we were engaged in a war (and Christians should know that they are) we would not expect to cower in our forts and defensive foxholes, afraid of the propaganda relentlessly showered upon us, when, just over the brow of the hill, the enemies' 'stronghold' turns out to be built on an indefensible position. So let's see how well their battle plans stack up, *or whether they even have any*. This is exactly the strategy applied by that chief of strategists, Jesus himself. He knew that the Pharisaic 'defensive' position was actually rotten to the core, being 'full of dead men's bones'. The particular worldview of the Pharisees, though apparently theistic, was in fact as non-theistic as could be, with a humanly-devised scheme aimed at controlling the masses, effectively enslaving them in what the Bible calls a 'works righteousness' instead of a 'faith righteousness'. If then we understand something of the amount of bluffing that goes on in ordinary, everyday conversation, let us proceed to find out more concerning where our particular protagonist is 'coming from'.

This is what I am calling the 'After-Dinner Chat Game'. The kind of after-dinner, across the table, open everyday conversation which all of us tend to engage in with family and friends. As the poker player calls the bluff of others, let's see what others say after we have shown them 'our hand', by insisting that they show us theirs. It may be that some of those who 'play with us' are indeed able to articulate the humanist position or some other worldview in great detail — but I would not bank on it. My money is on the fact that those who enter into such discussion will not have the slightest clue how to support their opening assertions beyond saying them out loud; that the minute you turn the tables on them, after making one or two bland statements, they are immediately out of their depth. As I have said, I (and countless other Christians) can articulate a position for days, if someone is prepared to let me. I would give *most* people no more than minutes before they begin to slip into an incoherent rhetoric and glib repetition (of things they have heard others say and not thought through themselves), with many going on to reveal their own illogical intolerance toward those who can articulate their beliefs.

Toward defining a worldview

It may be that by helping to elicit and construct a worldview in the 'After-Dinner Chat Game', where lightweight chat gives way to meaningful discussion, this will be the very first time that some have ever been faced with such a proposition. In my experience, discussions about worldviews often lead to different conversations entirely, avoiding the usual small talk and anti-theistic rhetoric.

So how do we actually go about this? I do not propose to set out any strategy that claims to be scientific. We don't need one. Neither do we need to force the issue. I am rather thinking of those many occasions that arise when matters of personal belief about life come up. Here are a handful of questions which go some way toward clarifying aspects of the worldview someone holds. And we should bear in mind that in discussions where our worldview is under attack, a whole bunch of 'don't knows', elicited when we turn the tables, are simply not good enough (when they have been freely attacking our worldview):

1. Where do you believe man came from?
- An accident of evolution.
- By design of a Creator God.
- Brought here by aliens from space.
- I have no opinion.

If the answer is, as is common, 'by accident of evolution', ask for their evidence. Chances are, the theory of evolution (for that is exactly what it remains, a scientific theory without a real basis in actual science) will be as foreign to their understanding as any theistic belief. They do not understand that 'the missing link' — the lack of a single bone revealing the transition of one animal type to another (which must have happened if evolution is true), is currently ruinous to their position. In other words, the evolutionist's position is as much built on faith as any theistic position — indeed more so, as it is built on blind faith.

I had assumed that one couple at a meal I attended would be evolutionists. When I asked the question however (arising out of the lady querying a programme she had seen on Christianity and other faiths) they actually believed aliens brought us here. I think they were more embarrassed by this assertion than we were. So I pressed the issue, only to hear that they could not explain why they believed this. It then had even less validity than the average evolutionist. I suspect it went back to reading the popular books of Eric Von Daniken in the 60s and 70s. The fact that von Daniken was later discredited, some of his 'evidence' having been fabricated to sell books and make money, was unknown to them.

2. Do you believe God exists? If you do, what is he like?
- Yes or no. a) a personal or an impersonal God. b) a God who cares or does not care about us/about you.

3. Do you believe in absolute truth?
- Yes or no.

If, for instance, there is no such thing as absolute truth, neither can there be any such thing as subjective truth. The liberal postmodernist believes that all truth is 'whatever is true for you'. But, following the postmodernist's own logic, this assertion itself cannot be true either. For truth to be subjective, it requires that there should be an absolute standard of truth (i.e. objective truth).

4. Do you believe in a 'gold standard' of morality?
- Yes or no.

Of course, if everyone holds different and individualized moral concepts, as the postmodernist and liberal usually do, then there can never be anything approaching true community or society or nationhood. By definition these things require an agreed, communal legal and moral consensus or code. Otherwise anarchy will reign.

For instance, all of us agree that murder is wrong. But if we have no gold standard of morality, how can murder possibly be 'wrong' for everyone? If all truth is relative or subjective, then even murder must, for some, be morally acceptable. But try telling that to the one being murdered. So then, if we set out to murder the liberal postmodernist and the anarchist, who reject the notion of absolute morality or a 'gold standard' of morality, they cannot complain, can they?

5. Who is the final arbiter of authority and truth in your life?
- My wife/husband/parent.
- I am.
- The civil/national authority.
- The Creator God and his Word (the Bible).

If ultimate authority lies with me, or even my family, how shall we ever concur, once again, with the notion of true community, society and nationhood which, because of human nature, needs to be controlled and subjugated by a legal code for the common good?

For these latter to exist harmoniously, we surely need to have an arbiter of truth above me and above my family members. Once again, if final authority does rest solely with me, then anarchy must surely rule beyond the area of my personal control and no one would be safe. If, as most might agree, final authority rests at the level of government for the common good, governing only by the will of the people (at least in a democracy), we know where its legal authority comes from, but from where does it receive its moral authority to govern?

6. Do you believe life has a purpose?
- To achieve personal happiness — to live for myself and my own pleasures.
- To procreate and live for my family.
- There is no real purpose.
- To know God and live for him.

If everything is pointless, why care about anything? But people do care. They care passionately about many things, not least their families, their personal achievements, leaving behind a legacy and making a 'mark' in the world. Ultimately, people are inherently 'programmed' to need purpose in their life. Yet most people will admit openly that life does not seem to have any real meaning or purpose — so they just make the best of it.

The theistic worldview answers all these big questions: revealing that, as created beings, we have our purpose in him who created us. All other worldviews both deny this truth and offer no hope in exchange.

7. Do you have a future hope for mankind?
- That man will master all things through scientific discovery.
- That man will achieve an earthly utopia and world peace.
- I have none — I just live for today.
- A world restored by the Creator God.

*If it is true that science will ultimately 'save' mankind from itself and its own destruction, with war vanquished and peace reigning forever, how is it that all science has been able to achieve so far is to reveal the 'how' of things, but **never** the 'why'? The 'how' indeed is the relevant question for science. But the 'why' remains a question for faith — and for faith alone.*

Many more questions could be posed. Indeed, you might add some of your own. The real point, however, is to help build a picture of how life and the world are generally perceived. The next thing is to pursue the logic of a particular belief, or whether it is just a presupposition based on 'what they had heard somewhere'. To be faced with the illogicality of many of our widely held presuppositions based on long discarded scientific theories, realizing perhaps for the first time that these presuppositions have been imbibed rather than 'believed', is quite often the first step on the path to questioning or changing our particular worldview. This is because the worldview of most people is a default, rather than a considered position. In other words it is a purely faith-based system — but one of the worst possible kind. It is a blind faith position lacking any real substance, evidence or reason (all of which, I would assert, the Christian theistic worldview patently has — as my bracketed comments indicate).

These questions, taken separately or collectively, are not

designed to be definitive or scientific. That would be to miss the point of the exercise entirely. But what they do is to broach the worldview question and reveal how ignorant most of us are about our own beliefs — and begin to get us to think more deeply about how intellectually we can justify them *to ourselves*, as much as to others.

It may be the first time that some have thought about this important subject. It may be that some who have been challenged in this way will simply opt out and choose the anti-intellectual path of continuing to persecute anyone who has the temerity to offer their views as absolutely true, while eschewing the identification and intellectual logicality of their own. If they are not prepared to enter into the validity of your questioning, then we may safely assume that they have disqualified themselves from making any serious observation concerning your views, not least in respect of your faith generally. But it is to be hoped that what is achieved is a level field for discussion of an issue which matters to us all: the pursuit of truth. Most of all it might help introduce into otherwise mundane and arcane 'table talk' a sense of purposeful realism which now understands that while science can tell us all 'how?', it is faith alone (and all worldviews, as we have seen, are faith-based) that can answer the much bigger question 'why?' At the very least, as Sire writes, 'to discover one's own worldview is a significant step toward self-awareness, self-knowledge and self-understanding'.[9]

Why a biblical worldview?

A biblical worldview is a pattern of belief that is biblically informed, being constructed from a series of key (as well as less key) doctrines of faith. In truth, it *ought* to be the position of each and every modern Christian. Sadly, it does not require a poll to reveal to us that it is not. Increasing numbers of those who refer to themselves as 'Christian' and who may attend church regularly, hold a syncretistic mix and match of beliefs, including some biblical and some humanly-devised philosophy. A growing number of modern Christians have even rejected a biblical worldview altogether. I will be perfectly honest that I am not interested here in concerning myself with either of the two latter positions. Both are incompatible with the mandate God himself has given for faith through his eternal Word written for us in the Scriptures. God in his Word is quite clear what it means to come to, and to grow in, faith. We are justified by faith alone, and continue to be sanctified (grow to maturity) by the renewal of the mind (Eph. 4:23), learning to discern 'empty philosophies' and the 'traditions of men' (Col. 2:8), 'holding fast the pattern of sound words' (2 Tim. 1:13) and ensuring that we are no longer subject to 'our understanding [being] darkened' (Eph. 4:18). Through this renewal of the understanding mind we are to relinquish our former ways of thinking and are now to be counted among those who do 'not think beyond what is written' (1 Cor. 4:6). Here in a nutshell is the call to develop and hold a biblical worldview: do not even *think* beyond what is written!

And nowhere is the whole divine purpose for holding a biblical worldview put better than in Paul's contention about the nature of the real human battle. That it is a spiritual battle, and one that, ultimately, is a battle for the mind. Put another way, we do in life what we believe. Paul puts it this way:

> For though we walk in the flesh, we do not war according to the flesh. For the weapons of our warfare are not carnal but mighty in God for pulling down strongholds, casting down arguments and every high thing that exalts itself against the knowledge of God, bringing every thought into captivity to the obedience of God (2 Cor.10:3-5).

The real spiritual battle in our world is the battle for the mind, not the heart (although that will be the corollary of winning the mind). The world teaches 'trust your heart'. This is not God's wisdom, however, but worldly philosophy. The great prophet Jeremiah warned explicitly not to 'follow our hearts' because 'the heart is deceitful above all things'. Following one's heart, if we would care to admit it with the cold light of experience, is the surest path to pain and failure. But win the mind and the heart will surely follow.

Forgetting the theological idiocy of the modern charismatic movement and the nonsense of the mystical books of Frank Peretti, the Bible's concern is not for spiritual 'Star Wars'-type battles adopting 'the force': rather they are battles for the spiritual understanding of the *material* mind — a mind that is able to engage with all sorts of worldly arguments which exalt themselves above God's eternal revelation in Jesus Christ, delivered to us in our Bibles. A mind that is able to 'pull down strongholds' (non-biblical patterns of thinking and belief — worldviews!) by sheer truth-telling. A mind so informed and taught by the Word of God that it can do no other than 'think biblically' as well as speak biblical truth. It will be a mind so captivated by the Word of God that it naturally refuses even to think 'beyond what is written' when it comes to godly truth, and is able to bring 'every thought into captivity to the obedience of Christ'.

It is plain enough, and we in the church must admit it, that the climate in the modern church is not Bible-based, nor 'of the mind' at all. The church in our generation is producing few great Christian thinkers. Indeed we are getting the leadership we deserve: a leadership that is wholly unable to bring a biblically-informed mind to apply God's Word to the modern world. We should have no doubt why the church in the West is in serious decline. It is not the Christian gospel which is any less relevant than ever it has been: rather it is because of the faithlessness of its modern leadership in teaching the biblical faith boldly, unafraid of offending men, being fearful only of offending God. In short, those who ought *most* to understand the need to teach a biblical worldview are often counted among those who do not even hold one.

The Scriptures speak to *every* area of life. First, Christians are no longer being taught the confessional patterns of belief of the historic church which make up its holistic basis of faith. Second, without such an holistic pattern of faith it is thoroughly ill-equipped to apply it faithfully and with biblical logic to the modern world. In the wake of the general deformation and fracture of the post-Reformation Bible-centred church, the modern Protestant believer has been allowed to so privatize his spirituality that it is hard to discern, in the hotchpotch of Bible truths and human philosophies being held, what a biblical and church worldview is.

If the need to expound a biblical worldview has become obfuscated in the modern church, the blame can squarely be laid at the door of our colleges, seminaries and the general church leadership. When all is said and done, if church leaders do not hold a biblical worldview when they leave their training colleges, then there is little hope of the average churchgoer being taught one either.

Fat bodies, fat minds
As we said at the beginning, each one of us consciously or subconsciously has a worldview[10] and acts and lives according to its values. It is a question of eliciting from ourselves, or from others, what that worldview is. This essay is not, as I have said before, a discussion on the various alternatives. For that discussion the reader is referred to worldview catalogues, such as the Sire book contains.

As a practising Christian, the state of the modern Christian mind (and particularly for me the Protestant and evangelical mind) is of considerable concern, as I confirm elsewhere in these essays. Though the modern Roman

Catholic Church is, in my view, in gross theological error in more ways than at the Protestant Reformation, it has unquestionably managed to retain something of a recognizable unity — a catholicity — across its spectrum. The same, sadly, cannot be said for the Protestant church, the church that was born of the sixteenth- and seventeenth-century Reformation by restoring the Bible and its worldview centre stage. As I point out in 'Why are so many Christians so gullible?', the state of the understanding and discerning mind of the modern Christian, church leader and academic theologian is today such that it has led directly to the growing impotence of the modern church. Now it may be here that the non-Christian reader will run out of patience as we are about to discuss the mind of the modern church and the *only* worldview to which it and all Christians are entitled: the biblical worldview. For anyone who is not interested in the internal state of the modern church, and does not want to understand what is happening to it at the dawn of the twenty-first century, by all means move on to the next essay!

It seems odd, even obscene, that in a world where hunger is prevalent, in the West obesity has become one of the biggest killers. It seems that hardly a day passes without the pros and cons of diets and proper bodily exercise being featured as major news items. The figures creeping ever upwards do not lie. Increasingly our society is killing itself by overeating. We eat the wrong kind of foods, and we exercise too little. A steady diet and regular exercise, and the obesity spectre would be slain with ease. But we have become comfort-eaters in an increasingly stressed, fast-paced world. We know this for a fact. But we would prefer to find a 'magic' pill to make things right for us, rather than cut down on our eating: something that would mean we could indulge our appetites as much as we like without paying the natural consequence of that self-indulgence. Such is the sloth and wickedness of the sinful human mind and nature. We insist on having it our way. We are good at demanding our rights, but not so quick to assume our responsibilities. It is a fact of history — something else most of us know little about — that all civilizations have foundered on such slothful, self-indulgent hedonism. Why should we expect ours to be any different? Here is human nature and a modern, anti-theistic, worldview in action.

For the Christian, however, obesity of body is not the only problem. Obesity of the mind has become an even more debilitating problem. For what we find in the modern church, especially in the West, is that human philosophies have supplanted biblical wisdom, not least in its Protestant form.[11] The results have been disastrous for the church. The consequences are plain to see. In village after village in rural England, where I live, we love to see the distinctive dreaming spires of our Norman-built churches. All sorts of people, not just church people, expend enormous energy on maintaining them. Meanwhile, the feeble morality and social gospel preaching coming from the pulpits of these same churches Sunday by Sunday, with fewer and fewer of their ministers teaching anything approaching a biblical worldview, results in their becoming centres for the aged traditionalists who can only vaguely remember why they keep going, though it is no longer for the biblical wisdom once expounded there. Of course, there is the modern 'evangelical', allegedly 'Bible-centred' alternative, which looks more like a (very bad) 70s variety show than a biblical church. In neither, however, are we likely to find biblically-informed worship and preaching, all geared to one end: teaching a biblical worldview.

I say again, the *only* worldview to which *any* Christian is entitled is a biblical one. God spoke to chosen men, prophets in the Old Testament era, and apostles in the new, to whom he gave eternal truth. They wrote down God's revelation knowledge, truth for all time. The New Testament scriptures gave birth to the *corpus Christi*, the body of Christ in the world, the church. Its purpose in the world is to preach forth that same revelation message in the gospel of Christ. In this way, the Christian faith is found in those same Scriptures and nowhere else. This is why Paul wrote to the church in Rome that 'faith comes by hearing, and hearing by the Word of God' (Romans 10:17). But we note that the Bible teaches that all of this is only possible if we are able proactively to understand or comprehend these things *by the renewal of the mind*. Let us be clear about what this means. The gospel of Christ is not something imbibed, nor is it something that comes to us 'spiritually' or by 'fanning a flame' already in us. This is pseudo-spiritual gobbledegook. The gospel comes to us externally from the Bible and is made real, brought alive, in us by the work of the Holy Spirit. But it comes to us fully by the conduit of God's choosing: the renewal and understanding of our minds. This is absolutely vital to grasp if we are not to pursue a Gnostic understanding[12] (an understanding which nearly destroyed the early church, such that the letters of John and others were partly written to counteract Gnostic influence). There are many modern Gnostics in various forms doing the spiritual circuit in our day.

If we are not to be counted among the Gnostics, mystics and countless others today who despise a faith which is, as the Bible requires, to be intellectually comprehended (understood by the mind), then all Christians will gratefully receive the biblical wisdom that God offers us. First, in serving him, second, in serving the common good — as God, biblically, determines that good. I am not here spreading the gospel that each of us needs to become 'intellectual'. But neither are we called to a mindless faith. You would not know it in the modern church, however. There is a culture of anti-intellectualism coursing through the veins of the modern world, and it has seeped into the body and culture of the modern church too. Individuals today, in our fast-paced world, no longer want to put the effort into thinking that they are perhaps prepared to put into their failing diets or gymnasium workouts. Most prefer the quick-fix pill method of avoiding thinking or applying their minds altogether, and thus, by default, allow others to do the thinking for them.

Fascinatingly, it is C.S. Lewis's Christian allegory in the *The Last Battle*, the last of the 'Chronicles of Narnia' series, which identifies the chief problem for 'decent' men being dulled by deceitful evil, as being the abrogation of their mental capacity. In short, the refusal to apply their minds and do what is right as a consequence. As the sly, self-serving monkey Shift says to the decent but naïve donkey Puzzle, 'You know you're no good at thinking, Puzzle, so why don't you let me do your thinking for you?'[13] And later on Shift gives his evil reasoning: 'It's because I'm so wise that I'm the only one Aslan [the king/Christ figure] is ever going to speak to. He can't be bothered talking to a lot of stupid animals. He'll tell me what you've got to do, and I'll tell the rest of you'.[14]

The average stated opinion, on almost any subject today, is not so much an informed opinion in the older sense at all: it is more akin to an emotional response. It is a common enough expression that 'I am entitled to my opinion'. True enough. But perhaps it ought to be an 'informed' opinion, at least. If it is not, though it may have the 'right' to be stated, it will not have the right to be received with equal weight, rightly or wrongly held. There is an assumption abroad that any opinion is morally equivalent to any other opinion. This is another manifestation of the postmodern worldview. I experienced something of this in practice over three years as a member of an Anglican parochial church council (PCC). We had accountants and solicitors and teachers on the PCC. When issues arose which touched upon things associated with each of those areas where we had 'in-house' expertise, such as from professionals in various walks of life, we quickly called upon that expertise. Oddly, however, whenever biblical expertise was called for (as most issues did) it was almost universally despised. Not in any overt way. But if Bible knowledge was called for, even the minister who was trained in it found it hard to have his voice heard. When it came to 'spiritual insight', it was as if it had become an anarchic free-for-all, with everyone thinking their view was as valid as anyone else's — whether they had biblical knowledge or not. This was because, and it is a widespread problem, spirituality is increasingly perceived as something 'bestowed' by the Spirit: not, as historically, biblical knowledge and understanding (which are truly bestowed by the Spirit).

Everyone, even the newest members, but especially those with the least Bible knowledge, would be the most vocal in asserting their 'opinion'. It was as if, while professional expertise mattered, Bible knowledge counted for little. And there is only one place at which we can point the finger for this parlous state of affairs: at the modern understanding of what church leadership means. For, as much Christian literature and pulpit teaching makes very clear, few church members today hold anything approaching a biblical worldview. And that should come as no surprise when church leaders themselves rarely hold one, either.

The crisis of leadership in the church

The Western church is in an extraordinarily advanced state of decline, having little coherent theology and having almost universally abandoned its biblical confessional heritage. In direct consequence, much of the modern church has no logical and reasoned pattern of belief to which it holds — and therefore no consistent biblical worldview to offer.

That the church has become irrelevant for many is as much to do with its confessional incoherence as its spiritual unfaithfulness. According to T. S. Eliot this should come as no surprise. In commenting on the nature of church leadership in the white English-speaking world, he says, 'the Anglo-Saxons display a capacity for *diluting* their religion, probably in excess of any other race'[15] (italics in original). Dilute what the church believes and teaches in common, of course, and we will have diluted the impact the Christian faith is likely to have. Pretty soon neither the church leader nor the church member will know what the church and they hold in common as truth. For the reality is that the Christian understanding is wholly dependent upon the renewal of the Christian mind, literally enabling that mind to see the world from a different point of view. We have already seen how even a tiny percentage of the Scriptures make exactly this point.

But it is also highly instructive to read through one of Paul's epistles, such as that written to the church at Phillippi, to begin to perceive just how deep this matter of the understanding of the mind is to Paul, and thereby to God himself. Right from the first chapter in Phillippians, Paul sets the tone by insisting that 'your love may abound still more in knowledge and all discernment' (1:9); that we 'stand fast in one spirit, *with one mind*' (1:27); 'being like-minded, of one mind' (2:2). We are called to 'work out' our own salvation 'with fear and trembling' (2:12). Paul laments that, at the time of writing, he has 'no one like-minded' (2:20); and desires that 'as many as are mature, have this mind' (3:15) and are 'of the same mind' (3:16). Believers are not to 'set their minds on earthly things' (3:19), but rather should 'be of the same mind in the Lord' (4:2), calling them also to 'guard your hearts and minds' (4:7). Have we got the message yet? The mind not only counts: without the mind's understanding our faith is less than worthless and our spirituality, in truth, more ephemeral than real.

With all this 'in mind' however, we are next called to judge/discern 'all things' (1 Cor.2:15, 6:2-3). And where our understanding was once 'darkened' (Eph. 4:18), now, through the renewal of the mind' (Eph. 4:23) and our determination 'not to think beyond what is written' (1 Cor. 4:6) — a widely ignored Scripture — our whole pattern of thinking is transformed. Now we are able to 'think biblically', wholly within a biblically-informed framework, and teach and preach a wholly biblical worldview.

The disgrace of our church age is that the majority of church pastors today simply do not hold a biblical worldview. Nor, in most cases, were they ever taught one in the academic training centres of our increasingly errant and church-divorced seminaries. Even those which do, teach a piecemeal and inconsistent, rather than harmonized, biblical pattern of faith. Dr Francis Schaeffer, once again, puts his finger right on the pulse when he states, 'Our theological seminaries hardly ever relate their theology to philosophy, and specifically to the current philosophy. Thus, students go out from the theological seminaries not knowing how to relate Christianity to the surrounding worldview'.[16]

In a recent survey of US Pastors, the Barna study group found that *only half* of Protestant pastors had a biblical worldview. In other words, half of all Protestant pastors and ministers have an understanding and view of the world which is not structured by God's unique revelation knowledge of it. Most have a pick-and-mix of biblical and other non-biblical worldviews. Citing the findings of the recently published national survey of 2033 adults, in a country where over half of the population claimed to have been in a church in the seven days prior to answering questions, less than 4 per cent of Americans claimed to hold a biblical worldview. The Barna survey itself found that 51 per cent of the Protestant pastors it questioned claimed to hold a biblical worldview. But as Barna rightly deduces, 'you can't give people what you don't have. The low percentage of Christians who have a worldview is a direct reflection of the fact that half of our primary religious teachers and leaders do not have one.'[17]

While the same Barna poll reported that there were significant differences among denominational groups[18], the most disturbing finding was that only 45 per cent of theologically trained seminary graduates had a biblical worldview. In stark contrast to this figure was the fact that 59 per cent of *non*-seminary trained pastors operated with a biblical worldview. What becomes glaringly apparent from this figure is that much of our Christian seminary training is actively working against future ministers holding and teaching a biblical worldview. Some of us have long been concerned at the increasing divorce of church and academy, with the latter and its leaders having little direct relation to the actual church 'on the ground'. When all is said and done, it is this, not the seminaries (as important as they should be) which matters most. Often entirely cocooned from the real world, the life of the academic who is separated from practising his theology through a local church (as men like Luther and Calvin did) is producing increasingly liberal and academic mindsets born of 'ivory tower theology', when what is needed is the straightforward 'street theology' (Bible application) of the apostle Paul.

The Bible speaks of the pastor/theologian as the one who is a 'right divider of the Word'. Though we would wish him to be well trained, this should not be at the expense of the gift of discernment, which is Bible-centred theology and the God-given ability to apply it. What is increasingly the case today is that many academic theologians have become irenic 'swats', endlessly prone to novelty and idle speculation, entirely divorced from the reality of church life. Such a picture is not reflective of every seminary and training college by any means. But it is perhaps fairly representative of the current culture of academic arrogance, as Barna's survey reveals all too clearly.

With such pastors and ministers in the pulpit, should we

be surprised that church members are left to flounder as to what they believe holistically, and are therefore able to apply in their daily lives? As Barna points out, 'Our research among people who have a biblical worldview shows that it is a long-term process that requires a lot of purposeful activity; teaching, prayer, conversation, accountability, and so forth.'[19] Given the increasing trend of schism, separatism and the growth of privatized religion among modern Christians, is it any wonder that the modern church is wracked by disunity? Is it any wonder that it is no longer able to present a coherent and logical worldview when neither the church, nor its members, align themselves to one either?

In an earlier survey Barna reported that 'a large share of the nation's moral and spiritual challenges is directly attributable to the absence of a biblical worldview among Americans'.[20] If the national survey to which Barna earlier referred, is correct, that only 4 per cent of Americans (and America is the last great Christianized nation in the Western hemisphere) have a biblical worldview as the basis of their moral and decision-making process, then there will undoubtedly follow severe consequences for the Western church. As Barna says, 'Behaviour stems from what we think — our attitudes, beliefs, values and opinions.' He goes on to point out that we in the church, just as those out in the world, are therefore, 'more concerned with survival amidst the chaos than with experiencing truth and significance'.[21] And we wonder why the church has grown steadily more incoherent and irrelevant in the world.

Os Guinness puts the case with the utmost clarity when he says, 'Anti-intellectualism is truly the refusal to love the Lord our God with our minds, as required by the first of Jesus' commandments. As God has given us minds, we can measure obedience by whether we are loving him with those minds (a key aspect of the First Commandment), and disobedience by whether we are or are not'.[22] Warning Christians of the consequences of this, Charles Malik said, 'The problem is not only to win souls but to save minds. If you win the whole world and lose the mind of the world, you will soon discover you have not won the world. Indeed it may turn out that you have actually lost the world'.[23] I would take his logic still further. Through our modern church techniques and methods, it is plain we are not impacting the world for Christ. Worse, those whom we do often draw in, are drawn not by the heart of the gospel which speaks of repentance from sin, but by a spurious 'Jesus loves you' message mixed with all sorts of other human philosophies. The cancer has spread in our generation throughout the academic seminaries and, worst of all, to the frontline pastorate.

Another poll seeking to adduce how American Christians were 'living their faith' today, recently found that less than half (49 per cent) believed that the Bible had any 'decisive authority' at all, with only just over a quarter (28 per cent) of respondents who claimed to bother regularly to study the Bible at all.[24] If the church is ever to regain its credibility toward God, let alone in the world, then it will need to become both confessional in its pattern of beliefs and to present, once again, a thoroughly reasoned biblical worldview to a world desperately in need of it.

Conclusion

Whatever our worldview, all of us should acknowledge that we live by one. The fact is that, as 'we believe', so 'we do'. Our beliefs govern our thoughts and our actions. Our core beliefs have a habit of working themselves out in all areas of our life. We commit our time and energy according to our pattern of beliefs. We owe it to ourselves, if not to others. That is, if we desire to be reasoned and logical people who profess to care something about truth, in ourselves and in others.

If however we are clear that we profess ourselves to be Christians, and we have never before thought of life in terms of an outworking of our worldview of it, let us grasp, as of first priority, that the Bible is not some two thousand-year-old 'spiritual devotional'. The Bible is nothing less than *the* handbook for *all* life. As Francis Schaeffer once put it, 'The Bible insists that truth is one — and it is the sole surviving system in our generation that does'.[25] Schaeffer believed this. Great scientists like Faraday believed this. Some of the greatest thinkers of the last two thousand years believed this. And they could all defend their beliefs. The question is this: what do you believe? And can you defend what you believe?

---

[1] James Sire, *The Universe Next Door: A Basic Worldview Catalog* (Leicester: IVP, 1988, third edition), p. 16.

[2] The postmodern worldview is perhaps, as we shall see, the most prevalent worldview of our age. Put succinctly, the postmodernist rejects the notion of absolute truth, believing that 'truth is whatever is true for each individual'.

[3] It is rightly said that 'liberals' are often the most illiberal and dogmatic of people. It is perhaps the height of irony that liberals are so often blind to the fact that their own beliefs are no less dogmatic than those which they denounce in others.

[4] For instance, it may suit me to have my local supermarkets open 24/7. But that means others have to work round-the-clock shifts, and often Sundays, to sustain 24/7 opening. It also means that those who live locally to a supermarket no longer have a break from the constant flow of traffic day and night.

[5] Sire, op. cit. p.16. Though, like me, Sire himself declares that he holds a biblical worldview, his book articulates the differences between all of the major worldviews. The book was originally written for, and widely adopted by, universities and students. Over 1,000,000 copies are in print.

[6] At least we can come up with a basic and coherent pattern. It will not be highly scientific nor exhaustive, but it will produce a 'whole' of a kind. The question of whether it will add up to a 'whole' which holds

intellectual, reasonable or logical water, is the real name of the game, however. What it can do, perhaps best of all, is reveal to many of us just how lacking in logic many of our worldviews actually are in practice.

[7] We should make no mistake. Faith in evolutionary theory — which is all it actually is! — is not based on a single fact of science. If there had been evolution of animal to man, or of one sort of animal type to another (and not just within the type), there should literally be millions of hybrid bones lying around to show it. The fact is that *not a single bone of this kind has ever been found* — 'the missing link' is still missing! If we are to be scientifically consistent, then we must realize (as many scientists actually do) that evolutionary theory remains just that, an unproven theory. Those who believe the theory therefore are individuals who 'hold a pattern of faith' just as much as do I — *except* that there is far more forensic and evidential proof for what I believe than for what they believe!

[8] Though, undoubtedly, one's worldview will be coloured radically according to which particular religion one adheres too.

[9] Sire, op. cit. p.16.

[10] That is to say that we have only one at a time. It is a fact of life that from time to time in our lives our worldview may change (such as when someone adopts the Christian or Islamic faith from a formerly humanist position, for instance — though I would still count humanism as a faith system).

[11] The signs for the Roman Catholic are not much better. Though Romanism maintains an appearance of far greater unanimity, it is largely only a façade, with priests on the ground and congregants living and doing according to their own particular worldviews, less and less informed by biblical doctrine.

[12] Gnosticism presents a dualistic understanding of the world (another worldview if you like): one which separates spirit and matter, seeing the former as 'good' and the latter as 'evil'. This is why countless modern Pentecostals and charismatics — along with the churches' many mystics — so despise the need for 'pure religion' or sound doctrine which all of the Scripture writers actually consider so important.

[13] C.S. Lewis, *The Last Battle*, (Glasgow: Fontana Lions, 1956), p.12.

[14] ibid., pp.32-3.

[15] T.S. Elliot, *The Idea of a Christian Society*, (London: Faber and Faber, 1939), p.25.

16 Dr Francis Schaeffer, from 'He is There and He is not Silent' in *Trilogy* (Leicester: IVP, 1990), p. 279.

17 George Barna, press release entitled 'Only Half of Protestant Pastors Have a Biblical Worldview', 12 January, 2004, on behalf of the Barna Group.

18 The breakdown of which revealed that the more 'Bible-centred' the denomination, the more likely it was for its ministers to have a biblical worldview.

19 Barna op. cit.

20 George Barna, press release entitled 'A Biblical Worldview Has a Radical Effect on a Person's Life', 1 December, 2003.

21 ibid.

22 Os Guinness, *Fit Bodies, Fat Minds* — a title I took some liberty with in the above article! — (London: Hodder & Stoughton, 1995) p. 18.

23 Charles Malik, *The Two Tasks* (IVP)

24 Gallup Poll entitled 'How are Americans Living Their Faith?', August 2003.

25 Dr Francis Schaeffer, 'The God Who Is There' in *Trilogy* (Leicester: IVP, 1990), p. 156.

ISSUES: Civil obedience & child discipline

8
The Limits of the Civil Law
(and its application in the spanking of children)

In December 2002, a group of independent Christian schools, led by Liverpool's Christian Fellowship School, failed in an attempt to get the British Court of Appeal to overturn a decision of the High Court which removed the right of schools to administer corporal punishment to pupils, even with parental consent. The action was brought on the grounds that the law breached the European Convention on Human Rights by interfering with the parental right to practise their religious beliefs.

In the event, the Court of Appeal upheld the earlier ruling. In doing so it noted that the right of parents to practise their religion was not infringed, as it still allowed *them* to administer corporal punishment to their own children if they misbehaved at school. While the Christian schools concerned are, at the time of writing, taking their case to the highest court in the land, the House of Lords (soon possibly to be replaced by a Supreme Court), by far the more important issue is how much longer parents will themselves retain the right to administer corporal punishment. The vocal lobby calling for a total ban has grown increasingly clamorous — even in the face of clear evidence of a burgeoning indiscipline problem in our schools. But what exactly is at stake, especially for Christian families, in this debate? While the argument for non-Christians revolves around the *temporal* issues of the alleged 'traumatizing' effects on children and parents, and the 'human rights of children', according to the Scriptures the issue of child discipline is no small one — linked as it is to the matter of *eternal* consequences. And in this context, it brings into sharp focus the whole issue of the rights of civil government over eternal matters, or, more prosaically, its boundaries and its duties when it comes to matters which have a higher, spiritual dimension altogether; matters which God has ruled upon and which it is not for the civil authorities to overrule — indeed those which the civil powers are obliged to protect.

The pressure to ban smacking
Under current British law it remains permissible for parents to administer 'reasonable chastisement' to their own children. State schools were banned from administering such punishment in 1986. That ban was extended to fee-paying schools ten years later. Incredible as it may seem, however, neither the Government nor the highly vocal 'anti-smacking' liberal lobbies make the link between the increasing violent indiscipline in our homes and schools and the progressively restrictive legislation that specifically precludes all forms of corporal punishment. While, for the moment, the British Government appears reluctant to remove the parents' 'right to smack' — no doubt aware of the fact that polls consistently reveal that most parents oppose such a move — lobby groups, including the highly vocal NSPCC, will accept nothing less than a complete ban. Indeed, if one listens to the conveyor belt of NSPCC spokespeople, one is in awe at their apparently congenital lack of ability to discern the difference between 'beating'

(as in causing bodily harm) and smacking or disciplining (as in administering proper chastisement) to children. The former is indeed perhaps the business of the NSPCC; the latter is in fact none of its business at all. The bigger issue, however, is that, if the Government does eventually bow to the pressure of the liberal lobbies — in conjunction with the pressure coming from already 'non-spanking' EU — how should Christian parents, indeed the church itself, respond?

Disciplining children: an underlying biblical principle

There is no question but that Christians are called to be the most law-abiding of citizens. Christian lives are to be the very model of holy living and obedience: first, before God as citizens of heaven; second, before all civil authorities as the Bible makes clear, 'Let every soul be subject to the governing authorities. For there is no authority except from God, and the authorities that exist are appointed by God (1 Peter 2:13-14). Therefore, whoever resists the authority resists the ordinance of God, and those who resist will bring judgment on themselves' (Rom. 13:1-2). And the reason too is made plain: 'For rulers are not a terror to good works, but to evil...He is God's minister to you for good'(vv.3-4).

But does this mean that laws passed by the temporal authorities are to be obeyed in *all* circumstances? What if, for instance, the civil authorities were minded to legislate to ban Christians — as Roman emperors did — from meeting together for worship? Are we bound to obey? Or, are we more likely to respond by answering to a higher authority and meet, as the early Christians did, in secret? What if sharing of the message of the uniqueness of Christ for salvation was formally banned? When tested on this very issue concerning the boundaries between divine and civil authority, Jesus proclaimed a very clear governing principle, 'Render therefore to Caesar the things that are Caesar's, and to God the things that are God's' (Matt.22:21). At a stroke,

Christ proclaimed that to obey 'Caesar' in all civil matters is to obey God himself (Rom. 13:3-4). Beyond that, however, he made it clear that in non-civil or spiritual matters, 'Caesar' had *no* jurisdiction other than to serve the best spiritual interests of God.

The parent-child relationship: a biblical perspective

The Fifth Commandment, and innumerable Bible passages associated with it, requires that children 'honour their parents'. And the Bible goes on to make abundantly clear what this means in practice: the instilling of obedience, backed by the threat and practice of physical force, if necessary. But it is the reasons given which alert us to the absolute necessity of not shirking this spiritual responsibility.

For a start we learn that 'Foolishness is bound up in the heart of a child, but *the rod of correction* will drive it far from him' in Proverbs 22:15. And, in the event that our sentimental modern minds should fail in this regard, we are told why it matters. 'Do not withhold correction from a child, for if you beat him with a rod, he will not die. You shall beat him with a rod, *and deliver his soul from hell*' (Prov. 23:13-14, italics added). By the very act of driving ungodliness from our children, born as they are in sin and needing instruction in righteousness, we are playing a supporting role with God in the child's sanctification, as a prelude to their justification. Though numerous other verses could be quoted, here is the heart of the issue. Discipline, backed if necessary by physical chastisement, is not only important for the child's general welfare, it is also *intimately bound up with the process which leads to the salvation of the soul*. We are told, 'train up a child in the way he should go, and when he is old he will not depart from it' (Prov. 22:6). Here is a command (train up a child) coupled with a promise (when he is old he will not depart from it). The unspoken truth here is that failure to obey this command may result in a dissolute life for which parents will, in part, because of their laxity, be held responsible.

A central purpose of proper child discipline, including physical chastisement, is then a vital component in forming godly character — part of the sanctification process which can help lead to personal salvation (justification) and growth (further sanctification). Both the old priest Eli (1 Sam.2:12-18) and King David himself (2 Sam.13f) had profound cause to rue their personal neglect of this biblical principle — and so should we. That some of their children turned out to be dissolute and godless, as the Bible makes very clear, is squarely down to their lack of disciplining in the home by their parents. Indeed, we should attempt to rid ourselves entirely of *sentimental* notions when administering discipline, if we are to be faithful, biblical Christian parents.

At the same time, we must add that the Bible does not, of course, sanction inflicting physical injury or abuse. As John MacArthur makes clear, 'Parental discipline should never injure the child. It is never necessary to bruise your children in order to...make your point. Spanking should always be administered with love and never when the *parent* is in a fit of rage...because it shatters the environment of living nurture and instruction Ephesians 6:4 describes'.[1]

The wickedness of 'evil by law'

The fact that God has appointed all civil authorities (Rom 13:1) is a long way from saying that all civil authority will duly obey him. Even so, the Scriptures, as we have seen, call us to submit ourselves to them in *all* temporal matters. But this does not extend to our submission to them in any eternal matters, however. Matters where, as we have already seen in relation to child disciplining, it simply has no jurisdiction. When the eternal conflicts with the temporal, then we are to obey God rather than men (Acts 5:29). The Psalms contain a number of warnings about temporal authorities who take it upon themselves to negate God's laws by creating barriers to godly citizens obeying God. The Bible calls this creating 'evil by law' (NKJV, Psalm 94:20) or, as the ESV puts it, 'fram[ing] injustice by statute'. In such instances we have no choice but to view such laws (no matter what lip-service we may pay to them in practice) as having no jurisdiction over us and act accordingly, the civil powers having exceeded their authority under God.

Perhaps, in passing, we should also note the serious consequences for those who play a part in enshrining such unbiblical 'evils' within the civil laws of the land. As the Bible makes clear, the devisers of 'evil by law' will, come Judgment Day, pay a terrible price (Psalm 94:20-23). Politicians, particularly Christian politicians, beware!

Conclusion

The righteous role of schools in helping to administer good and proper child discipline has in our generation, sadly, been greatly diminished. But our major concern now ought to be for the preservation of the right of *all* parents the right to chastise and spank their own children, when they deem it necessary. As the Bible quaintly points out, 'After all, it won't kill them' (Prov. 23:13, I paraphrase). In the smacking and proper chastisement of children then, as in all matters there the civil law must not overstep its bounds, the Christian may well be called to civil disobedience for the sake of the gospel of Christ. As Francis Schaeffer puts it in his discussion on the subject of civil disobedience:

> God has ordained the state as a *delegated* authority; it is not autonomous. The state is to be an agent of justice, to restrain evil by punishing the wrongdoer, and to protect the good in society. When it does the reverse, *it has no proper authority*. It is then a usurped authority and as such it becomes lawless and is a

tyranny...The bottom line is that at a certain point it is not only the right, but the duty, to disobey the state.²

In view of all that has been said here, I have little doubt that the case brought by the Christian schools, at the head of this essay, that the ban on smacking by teachers in schools 'breaches the parents' right to practise their religion' is actually an ill-advised one. What it does immediately, if they were to win their case, would be to create different categories of rights for those within the church and those outside it. As we have seen, however, it is the God-given right of all parents, Christian or non-Christian, to chastise their children with the occasional smack. The church is *not*, or ought not to be, in the business of going cap in hand to the state to allow it special dispensations in moral matters: rather it should be in the business of seeing to it that the civil powers understand their responsibilities and their limitations and, just like Pilate, from whom their power derives. This will often mean arguing the logic of the moral position, as well as the blatant *illogic* of a position which denies the right to discipline in a climate where child discipline in the home and the school is at breaking point.

But whatever the civil authorities may or may not do, the Christian parents' abiding concern and first duty is to fear God, not the strictures of men. God instructs us all to obey the civil law at every point *except* where it conflicts with his eternal laws, and there are plainly serious spiritual consequences, both temporal and eternal, attached to Christ's oft-quoted 'render unto Caesar'. In these consequences we are able to discern the sheer depth of God's love for us as his children, and ours for him as our own Father — and we would do well to perceive our own relationship with our own children in this same loving light.

Happy too the children so trained in habits of obedience to their earthly parents that they learn almost instinctively to obey and honour God. He [Hudson Taylor's father] felt...that Christian parents are placed at the head of the family as the direct representatives of Him 'from whom every fatherhood in heaven and on earth is named'. To permit disobedience would be not only unfaithfulness to God, but cruel injustice to the children, wholly misleading them as to the character of the Heavenly Father with whom through life they have to do. His duty on the contrary was to train them to such prompt and loyal obedience to their earthly parents that they would be prepared to render like submission to the will of God...such obedience requires the exercise of the highest powers, faith, love, patience, self-control, and is a faculty not easily acquired. Unless they learned the lesson in childhood, they would grow up with unyielded wills, too wayward and undisciplined to be of use in the service of God.

from *The Biography of Hudson Taylor*

---

[1] John MacArthur, *Successful Christian Parenting: Raising Your Child With Care, Compassion, and Common Sense* (Nashville: Word, 1998), p. 155.

[2] Dr Francis Schaeffer, essay on 'The Limits of Civil Obedience' in *A Christian Manifesto* (Wheaton, Ill: Crossway Books, revised edition 1982), pp. 91 and 93.

ISSUES: Media morality & abortion

9
When TV Gets the Morality Right

I am a big fan of the US TV series *CSI Miami*.[1] The concept behind CSI is that, in the case of more heinous crimes such as homicide, it is less the detecting abilities of the old-style 'gumshoe' and more the hard-nosed forensic work of the police science laboratory which solves the crime in the 21st century. Filmed using the latest computer graphic techniques, it aims to reveal, in occasionally harrowing yet compelling clarity, something of the effect of bullets, chemicals and explosions on the human body and other objects. It is little wonder that the series has regularly found itself in the top ten viewing lists for the last couple of years and with the occasional TV Emmy Award thrown in.

Another thing that is impressive about this fifty-minute modern take on detectives with science degrees is its propensity to deal with difficult issues, including the failures of the justice system itself. Even with the aid of the incredible strides made by modern forensic science, the occasional *known* perpetrator cannot be prevented from 'walking' (hardly the happy-ending syndrome favoured by the Hollywood film machine). But it is in the minutiae of the storylines and the relentless pursuit of objective, forensic truth that, just occasionally, we glimpse a little more depth than is found in the average cop thriller.

God in the works?
One of the attractions of this science-based programme is the regular insight we receive into the laws of forensic science — laws which bear (and they will, won't they) the hallmark of design by a higher power; a power which can mitigate even the grossest evil and secret designs of human 'wisdom'.

Take, for instance, the episode where our hero awaits outside a grand suburban house as his friend and bomb-squad officer colleague defuses a necklace bomb.[2] In fact the real target in this episode turns out not to be the 'necklace' victim *per se*, but rather the bomb-defusing team itself. When the worst happens and the bomb explodes, killing both the bomb disposal officer and the necklace victim, we witness, in slow motion, the spectacular impact as the front windows of the house shatter and blow out.

But it is as part of the ensuing investigation that we learn an interesting and important fact about bomb explosions — the preferred weapon of the modern urban terrorist. As a member of the investigation team explains to a colleague, bomb explosions have two phases. The first carries much of the bomb material, and other objects surrounding it, away from the vicinity of the detonation. This causes a vacuum to develop at the seat of the explosion, setting up a second phase which draws much of the debris back into the original detonation area. This is very important, as it means that what would otherwise be a massive crime scene area, with its essential clues which can aid in discovering the all-important 'signature' of the bombmaker, is thus vastly reduced, aiding the subsequent investigation enormously. As this was being explained, the slow motion re-run graphically illustrated its truth by focusing on an unfortunate domestic bird (no doubt a fake) which is first hurled through the window only to be sucked back through it again in phase two.

What came home is how the natural laws often operate pro-actively to aid those pursuing truth and justice in identifying those responsible for crime. Even the cleverest of bombmakers, it seems, are now forced to run the gamut not only of state of the art detection techniques, but also our greater understanding of the laws of nature, laws by which all of us are governed. As a Christian, it is hard not to detect something of the hand of God in this small example of the two-phase explosion process which ultimately enables justice to prevail. Good may yet come out of even the very basest of murderous evil.

In many of the CSI shows, but especially the Miami version, there have been many key moments which suggest a moralism to the show, especially in the lead character, Lt Horatio Cain (played by the excellent David Caruso), who is driven by an overweening sense of truth and justice to get to the heart of the matter, no matter what. Now I do not for one minute suggest (as I simply do not know) that the producers and writers of *CSI Miami* are specifically setting out to make, subliminally or otherwise, powerful moral points. What I do think is that whenever *objective* truth and logic are employed and pursued, as here through real (not popular) science, to their natural conclusion, moral godly truths have a 'nasty' habit of revealing themselves. Let me give a prime example of what I mean by reviewing briefly another *CSI Miami* episode, one where its scripted assertions and observations concerning abortion, ran counter to the prevailing, liberal-dominated, attitudes of modern TV culture.

Is it a baby, or is it a fetus?
In the first season's episode 'Ashes to Ashes', we learn that a wealthy man has brutally murdered his unconscious pregnant girlfriend by driving her car into the river, causing her

to drown. Later we discover that the sick and cynical motive for the murder was simply that his girlfriend's pregnancy would have 'cramped his lifestyle'.

That the leading CSI, Horatio Cain, is visually upset by the death not only of the mother but of the unborn child, is quickly established. That he is equally determined to employ all the forensic evidence he needs to 'get this man', also becomes apparent. What is particularly moving is Cain's compassionate pursuit of justice, not only on behalf of the murdered adult, but on behalf of a murdered *seven-week-old* child. Think about it for a moment, only seven weeks old. In the parlance of today's pro-abortion world, seven weeks barely registers as a child at all. That the programme had no compunction about treating the death of such a young 'unborn' in the womb as of *equal concern* with the death of the mother, and refusing to adopt the contemporary ruse of using the less emotive word *fetus*[3] for 'baby', is novel on prime-time TV. It would have been just as easy for the writer or producer to make the pregnancy a lot more advanced, creating perhaps an even greater sense of melodrama at the loss. But who in today's mass media, with its blatantly liberal ethos, considers a seven-week-old as a baby? The fact that it *did* give the baby the respect for its human status which it deserved, spoke volumes about how the mass media almost always fails to accord the unborn its true status, and gave a powerful, perhaps unwitting, message to any 'pro-choice', in reality, 'pro-abortionists', watching.

After all, who today would be bothered concerning the loss of a seven-week-old 'undeveloped' fetus? Given Western society's propensity to treat young life in the womb as having almost no human rights, as the 'pro-choice'[4] brigade do, even up to the age of 24 weeks, this was a refreshing change indeed. But the reality of the pain attached to *all* early human death, even death at seven weeks, was about to be crystallized when Cain requests that the dead fetal tissue (the body) be removed from the mother's corpse. The pathologist, acceding to the request, notes that performing this activity was one of the most distressing she ever had to do.

Next, the pathologist having complied with his request, we see Cain in his laboratory viewing the now deceased seven-week-old under the microscope — and we are allowed to see for ourselves the very formed, even at seven weeks, dead baby. Visibly moved to the edge of tears by what he sees, Cain has to leave the room to compose himself. It is only later that we realize his true purpose in all this. When the forensic and other evidence prove to be insufficient to charge or prove the guilt of the perpetrator, the killer and his lawyer arrogantly make to leave police custody. But Cain stands in front of him and holds up to his face a picture. It is a composite picture of a little girl — a mock-up prepared by laboratory colleagues. 'This', says Cain slowly and very deliberately, 'is your daughter as she would have looked on her second birthday had you not killed her and her mother'. Now Cain's action did nothing to prevent the killer from 'walking'. But what it achieved, and very dramatically, is the reality of what it means to murder an unborn child in a singular and powerful screen moment. It portrayed the truth that a seven-week-old fetus *is* indeed a baby, a human child. Just as Cain himself perceptively and gently observed as the dead fetal tissue was earlier being removed: 'Not just skin cells, is it?' No indeed, it is not.[5]

I have no reason to believe that the programme makers were set on making a specifically anti-abortion case here, but it was as good and clear and dramatic an instance in support of the anti-abortion case, as I have witnessed on prime-time TV in a long time. In the world of the liberal-minded, amoral, often immoral, culture of entertainment-dominated mainstream TV, when the medium does occasionally get the

God-given morality right, it can yet make for powerful broadcasting — and Christians should be gracious enough to say so.

And when it comes to the much more important issue of abortion generally, though there are some difficult issues involved on occasions, each one of us needs to know that God has already spoken on the matter thus:

> *Before I formed you in the womb I knew you;*
> *before you were born I sanctified you.*
> **Jeremiah 1:5**

In the modern, often vacuous, debate over the issue of when a child becomes a child, God has made the matter very clear. It is illogical and odd, is it not, how some people will one moment happily treat the baby in the womb, right from conception, lovingly as 'the baby'; and how, the moment it is unwelcome or in some way burdensome, it reverts, inexplicably, to becoming 'a fetus' and something to be disposed of at the earliest opportunity? A perverse people, are we not; a people who do indeed have a natural propensity to suppress the truth of God (Romans 1:18); that 'professing to be wise, they became fools' (v.21)? But such *is* the mindset of the uninformed, the uncaring and the self-serving.

---

[1] CSI – Crime Scene Investigator. *CSI Miami* is a spin-off from the original CSI series set in Las Vegas. For me, the balance of scientific logic and the high premium placed on 'truth', mixed with occasional bouts of a genuine compassion expressed through the lead character, Horatio Cain, is where the Miami version scores over the original. At the time of writing, *CSI New York* is yet to get under way.

[2] A bomb placed around an individual's neck that can explode with the merest sudden movement (a device favoured by some terrorists).

[3] *Fetus* is merely the Latin word for 'baby'.

4 It is a constant practice among those of a liberal mindset to obscure the truth of the matter by devising more socially 'acceptable' language. Thus 'pro-choice' (which is meaningless) is preferred to the more controversial 'pro-abortion' (which is more appropriate). We should *not* let them get away with this practice.

5 The duplicity of much liberal thinking never fails to amaze me. The same liberal couple who are excited at the prospect of an impending birth, get excited referring to the unborn as 'the baby', even as 'little Joe' or 'little Beth', can just as easily, given it is an 'inconvenient' pregnancy, instead describe the unborn in the wife's womb as 'the fetus', denying that it is yet a baby at all!

ISSUES: Anti-Semitism & Christian evangelism

10
(Observations on the issues surrounding)
Mel Gibson's *The Passion of The Christ*

***Part I (a socio-political perspective)* —
*Is it anti-Semitic?***

Not since Martin Scorsese's *The Last Temptation of Christ* has a film stirred up as much controversy as Mel Gibson's *The Passion of the Christ*. What has marked out Gibson's offering as most controversial — and animated public debate as never before — has undoubtedly been its graphic portrayal of violence and murderous intent of first-century Jewish religious authorities.

It is perhaps a sign of our postmodern times that what has so upset some critics is not whether the violence shown reflects reality or transgresses artistic 'good taste', but whether it will serve to inflame modern anti-Semitism. Interestingly, not one critic seems to be concerned about a similar outbreak of 'anti-Italianism', given that Jesus suffered (as the film graphically depicts) appalling brutality at the hands of Roman soldiers. But let us not allow logic to spoil a good controversy.

The case against Gibson, being a member of a strict sect within Roman Catholicism which has apparently made anti-Semitic remarks in the past, is that Gibson himself has set out to make a specifically anti-Semitic film. It should however be plain to most objective observers and to those who have heard Gibson himself that such a view is simply not viable. Indeed, it grossly underestimates Gibson's openly-espoused and repeatedly stated motivation for making the film: that he is a man so overawed by the person and atoning sacrifice of Jesus Christ that he was driven to make it. But, frankly, it is difficult to understand why such an accusation can be levelled at all.

The New Testament (authored mostly by Jews) carries the spoken and self-condemning line, 'Jesus' blood be upon us and upon the heads of our children'. Gibson includes this admission in his film. It is a line which, in its repetition, does two things. It reveals graphically how far the OT Judaistic religion had so obscured the truth of God that it could not even recognize God's own Son; and it would, in its biblical retelling, always leave the 'teller' open to a charge of anti-Semitism — especially by those unable to distinguish between 'Jewish-ism' (nationality) and 'Judaism' (the old Judaistic religious understanding). It is this distinction which the Bible, and the Christian church, seek to communicate. However, this does not prevent the church's detractors (nor confused evangelical dispensationalists!), in their ignorance, confusing the issue and serving their own ends. Significantly, though the line is actually spoken in the film in the original Aramaic tongue (the language of the whole film) Gibson himself chose not to translate this line in the on-screen subtitles. Refusing to include the most self-condemnatory, potentially 'anti-Jewish' of lines is hardly the action of a man bent upon anti-Semitic ends.

In the current debate there is something altogether incongruous, even shabby, in the various attacks of the vocal liberal lobbies concerning Gibson's true motives. Instead of pointing the 'anti-Semitic' finger where it really needs to be pointed — at the blatant and vicious source of most modern anti-Semitism: the Islamic militant movement and various Arab states — they choose instead the soft target of a retelling of the gospel story. It should however be widely acknowledged that those who regularly espouse distinct anti-Semitic views, need no 'Christian' film to fuel their ignorance and hatred.

In attempting, in the course of just two hours seven minutes, to depict all the salient elements and emphases of Christ's Passion, one would have thought that any film-maker, even the most biblically correct (and Gibson is not) would struggle to fulfil such a lofty aim. The limitations of film, of course, much like any literature or artwork, can, at best, provide only a one-dimensional version of the story, being forced to miss out much meaning and explanation and adopt necessary artistic licence. That is precisely why God himself made preaching, *and no other medium*, the chief means for the propagation of the Christian gospel. No film, no book, no work of art, can be a substitute for *preaching*, the means by which the church is mandated (no matter how much modern Christians might think they have come up with better ways) to communicate the gospel. If anyone, or any church or church leader, therefore, thinks that Gibson's film can *do* a better job of evangelism than the church, then they should think again (see part II).

Whilst it is undoubtedly true that Jews and Romans brought about Jesus' death, the higher truth for Christians, as for Gibson's film, is that it was God himself who was ultimately in control of the events of the Passion. And thus it was God himself who orchestrated Jesus' death with his Son's full compliance.[1]

Who *actually* killed Jesus?

Who actually put Jesus to death is clear from the gospel accounts, other records and Gibson's film. It was the Roman authorities who finally condemned him to death by crucifixion (as much as Pilate might have liked it to appear otherwise) and who carried out the act itself. But, as Gibson's 'Jesus' states, the 'greater sin' or responsibility, *in human terms*, rested with the Jewish authorities *acting in their authoritative religious* (i.e. Judaistic) capacity. It was they, not the Romans, who concocted false charges and ultimately 'handed him over' for condemnation, for which the death penalty was, by Jewish law, decreed. If this is to be construed as anti-Semitism, then it is inherently written into the gospel accounts and thereby the teachings of the historic church. Jewish liability was 'the greater' for the simple reason that to the Jews, as a chosen OT people, had specifically been given the 'oracles of God' — and therefore they, unlike the gentile Romans, were without excuse. Separating out the guilt borne of the man-made traditions of the Judaistic religion (which Christ had continually rebuked) from those of a Jewish national identity has always proved a struggle for some. When they, like many modern dispensationalists, hear remarks against non-biblical traditions of Judaism, they mistakenly associate being Judaistic with being Jewish. The erroneous and baseless accusation of 'anti-Semitism' then is made out of ignorance.

That the first-century Jews, primarily, and the Romans, secondarily, were collectively responsible for the wicked injustice suffered by Christ is an irrevocable fact of history. By calling for bans and boycotts of artful and literate forms of the story's retelling — something I expect to see more of in the future — liberals and leaders of modern Judaism alike (of course, the latter has a *religious* stake in denying the gospel message) are simply revealing their own inherent phobias. In this case 'Christophobia', an increasingly pervasive sickness in Western culture. If they term the Christian message 'anti-Semitic', then they will have to do a proper job and ensure the closure of *all* churches and ban the proclamation of the preaching of the gospel inside, as well as outside, church walls. But then, as the Bible makes clear, the *ultimate* responsibility for the events surrounding the Passion rests neither with the Jews nor the Romans, but with God himself. Gibson himself understands this.

Who, *ultimately*, was/is responsible for Jesus' death?

For any who choose to go and see Gibson's film, there is one highly significant 'on-screen' moment that should tell us everything we need to know about Gibson's belief concerning *who* is most responsible for Christ's death. As Jesus is being nailed to the cross, the film focuses in slow motion on a single pair of hands which proceed to hammer home the enormous nails. These hands belong to Mel Gibson. This is no ordinary, Hitchcock-style, cameo role for Gibson. This is Gibson making a very profound statement. A statement which contends: if you are looking for someone to blame for this heinous act, *blame me* — and blame yourself. For, Gibson clearly believes, it is *his* sins, *my* sins, and yours dear reader, which meant the inevitability of God's self-sacrifice if they were to be expunged — an action 'choreographed' by God himself in the events of the Passion.

In this, Gibson confirms the very heart of the Christian gospel, the preaching of faith in Christ's atonement for our sins. Where historically some have perpetrated the vilest acts against Jews, sometimes sadly in the name of the Christian faith, it was plainly done in ignorance and rejection of the New Testament teaching concerning forgiveness, *not out of obedience to it*. To claim that Gibson, through his film, is set on fuelling modern anti-Semitism by retelling these critical events is as absurd as claiming that the church today holds the modern state of Israel (or Italy for that matter!) responsible for carrying out the act. As Gibson well knows, we *all*, every one of us as sinners, bear a responsibility here.

Whatever the theological nuances, or potentially even bizarre beliefs, of the group to which Gibson belongs, he himself undoubtedly understands that it is human sin — the unrepented sins of us all — that necessitated the death of Christ, in the salvific redemption plan of the Father. Though the modern, obsessive politically-correct liberals might like to rewrite, or obfuscate, the facts of history in an attempt to cover up this truth, we must not let them. They would be better occupied addressing the more obvious seats of anti-Semitism today. But then that would be politically incorrect — and personally dangerous.

Though in Gibson's film we graphically witness ancient Jewish leaders calling for Christ's death and ancient Italians knocking in the nails, we do well to remember, as Gibson well understands, that the Bible's assertion is that the each one of us bears a responsibility for necessitating this *divine* action. Bluntly put: we may as well have held the hammer ourselves. In short, the charge of anti-Semitism does not stand up.

As I exited onto the High Street from my local cinema, I mused about the views of the people rushing about their business, and postmodern man's diffidence toward claims of absolute truth. The whole notion of pogroms on the streets brought about by Gibson's film seemed as far-fetched as any movie fantasy. If we, as a nation, are serious in our desire to locate genuine sources of often murderous anti-Semitism, the focus of our attention ought not to be extremists in local cinema-going audiences, but rather the Islamofascists who are resident in some local mosques. If you think that too harsh an indictment — there undoubtedly being many solid citizens who frequent mosques — consider this: the central message of Islam and the Koran (read it for yourself) is to call upon believers to 'kill infidels' (by which it means Jews and Christians) and 'die for the prophet' (an implicit incitement to martyrdom). The central message of the Christian church, however, is that 'Christ died for you' and 'love your enemies'. We can choose to ignore the appalling reality of the relentless Islamic persecution of Jews and Christians as much as we like. But it will not change the fact of it one jot.

Part II (a Christian perspective)—
Is it good evangelism?

Numerous evangelical and Roman Catholic churches block-booked cinema seats during the opening weeks of *The Passion of the Christ* both in the USA and the UK. Though most went to see the film for themselves, many saw it as a major evangelistic opportunity and invited family members and friends. Gibson's film has received wide acclaim from Roman Catholics and evangelicals alike. A minority of evangelicals, however, concerned (as this writer is) for biblical veracity, expressed reservations. Some claimed it was blasphemous for having extra-biblical scenes, and others disliked the Roman Catholic emphasis. But the most serious charge was that, by depicting Jesus at all, the film was guilty of contravening the Second Commandment, which forbids the making of images of God.

There is no doubt among the more biblically-minded that Gibson's film lacks biblical integrity at a number of points. Gibson has undoubtedly given the film a Roman Catholic 'gloss' with its unbiblical extra emphasis on Mary and other kinds of extra-biblical 'licence'. In that sense, *The Passion* cannot claim to be totally faithful to Scripture nor, therefore, 'the best kind' of evangelism. But some reviews I have read simply undermine their own credibility by

The Politics of Faith

bolstering their assessments with unfair criticism. One, for instance, alleges: 'Nowhere is Christ identified as the Son of God'. Not true. The film actually carries the scene where Pilate asks: 'Are you the Son of God?', 'Jesus' answers with the straightforward and biblical reply (the words being written on the screen): 'I AM. And you will see the Son of Man coming ...', etc. Clearly this particular critic had been out buying popcorn at the time.

Others were concerned that 'nowhere' did the film clarify 'what all the suffering and blood were for'. Yet, in this writer's remembrance, it was made perfectly clear and in a number of different ways. In this respect the film also benefited from being spoken in the Aramaic language of Jesus. This in turn had the beneficial consequence (for those of us more Word-orientated) of a good deal of Scripture appearing on the screen. This too goes some way to negating the criticism of some that the film's emphasis on the violence accorded to Jesus (which, though it undoubtedly took place, is *not* the emphasis of Scripture itself) meant that the film was purely about powerful images, not scriptural truth.

The problem, however, is that most modern evangelicals readily heaped uncritical acclaim upon the film. Fairly representative is this quoted in America's *Christianity Today* magazine: 'Gibson's *Passion* is "the greatest outreach opportunity in 2000 years".' This, in view of the film's already mentioned shortcomings, has led in turn to a swift backlash, with some going overboard in their response. But it was the nature of the arguments themselves that caught my attention. If nothing else, the disputation among evangelicals highlighted the 'grey' area where Christianity and culture juxtapose and overlap, and especially the conflicts that may or may not arise in consequence. For those wholly inculcated into the evangelical entertainment culture, pretty much anything goes anyway, so any film that gets people talking would do (even if featuring heresy and blasphemy).

For my own part, I am far more concerned with those who claim to be Bible-believing but have rather substituted their own tradition, alleging that *all* modern culture is secular, ungodly and unchristian. It seems to me that there is a real need among allegedly Bible-believing Christians today to recover what it means to be 'in the world, not of it', without turning it into a fear-filled travesty of being 'not of the world — and hiding from it'. '*In it*, not of it' means *fully* engaged with it. But, if we are, as a contemporary church community, to begin to re-engage with all aspects of the culture and society around us, we shall need to lose our fear of men, and modern man's culture. At the present time most Bible-believing Christians can be defined by what they are against, rather than what they are for — or *not* against.

By doing so we might yet learn to discern better where the cultural lines should be drawn, and where we might be more relaxed about things. This would also help us to relate to our world, whether we express agreement with it or not. It would also help us to understand the nature of that liberty to which Christ has freed us. Paul addressed this issue specifically at 1 Corinthians, chapters 8 to10, when he spelled out the principles of Christian liberty, especially as it applied to the 'weaker brother' syndrome which, as we shall see, is highly relevant here. This becomes even more apparent as we learn that not even those biblically-minded, Reformational pastors and theologians who might perhaps be relied upon to give us more definitive biblical guidance in the case of Gibson's film, are unable to do so.

A Reformational debate on the merits of *The Passion*

As good Bible-believing Christians then, where might we expect to receive more informed theological debate on the subject of Gibson's film? The Internet has been buzzing with the wholesale lauding of the film — and its wholesale condemnation, too. Well, perhaps I could direct the reader to a debate in the pages of the excellent *Modern Reformation* magazine. *MR* is the magazine of the Alliance of Confessing Evangelicals in the USA, an alliance of leading, Bible-believing, Reformational churches, pastors and theologians.[2] The May/June 2004 issue of *MR*, 'A Good Church is Hard to Find', gave its 'Between the Times' section to a forum for seven well-respected, mostly Reformed, theologians to give their opinion on the spiritual merits or otherwise of *The Passion*.

Perhaps the most definitive observation we could make concerning that particular debate is ... that it was inconclusive in its findings. If the debate proved anything, it was that we struggle to be able to apply the Scriptures in areas where Christianity v. culture overlap — and that, quite often, our view need not be for or against, but nuanced or even neutral. It is fair to say that the only uniform opinion expressed in the debate, and one this writer shares, is that Christians generally should not approach this, or any, film uncritically. Within that, a variety of differing and opposing opinions were expressed. Take for instance the prime 'anti' position (and the overriding objection from some evangelicals) that the film was guilty of breaking the Second Commandment in its depiction of Jesus. Pastor/theologian Mark Dever of Capitol Hill Baptist Church, Washington DC, asks rhetorically, "Where do I stand on this? I am not certain'. He goes on to explain why: 'Many conservative Protestants have long made exception for temporary pedagogical representations — like Sunday school skits or Campus Crusade's *Jesus* film. We don't intend to use these images for worship.' He is absolutely right. A film has nothing to do with worship, and it is the issue of worship with which the Second Commandment is primarily concerned, as any careful reading of Exodus 20:4 makes clear. The historic church has long understood this. Biblically appropriate visual representations of Jesus (who is both the image of the

Father as well as fully man) when presenting the gospel message have never troubled the church. I would go further. Thousands actually saw the face of Jesus when he went about his earthly ministry. They would have carried that 'image' of God the Son around with them post-Calvary for the rest of their lives. Was the retaining of that image in their heads, knowing Jesus was God, really going to bring them under condemnation according to the terms of the Second Commandment?

Returning to our *MR* debate, even the normally highly astute Douglas Hart presents an illogical pattern of thinking in putting forward the 'violation of the Second Commandment' (assuming it, rather than arguing it) as his chief reason for eschewing the film. However, the same writer also makes this assertion: 'I [also] like to be entertained sometimes...by the qualities that film possesses uniquely and by a good story or intriguing character. I guess *The Passion* could qualify.' On the one hand he maintains Gibson has broken the Second Commandment. On the other he suggests that the film could qualify (I infer from this) as viewable material within a 'cultural' context. While I fail to see the logic of the position, I do agree with what Hart is getting at, which I believe is central to the whole discussion.

The debate surrounding Gibson's film has perhaps been confused somewhat by Gibson's own articulated statements — as well as the overtly violent nature of it, which has shocked some. In this we would be right to question a man who is no theologian, nor a pastor, but simply 'a believer' with the power (and professionalism) to reflect his 'personal take' on the biblical Jesus, on celluloid. This is no different, it seems to me, from any church member publishing a book giving his or her own 'take'. It may be flawed, but is it necessarily blasphemous because of those flaws? Ultimately, such books — or such films — may or may not reflect the only 'take' that really counts — Scripture. But it does not necessarily mean that it is either blasphemous or idolatrous, depending of course on the nature of that 'flaw'. Let us for the moment forget Gibson and his motives and allow the film to stand, as it ultimately will, in a cultural context only.

Though David VanDrunen, Professor at Westminster Seminary in California, states that his 'Reformed understanding of the Second Commandment' is his chief objection to the film, once again the case is not argued, and it is difficult to see from where in Scripture the assertion can be supported. Another contributor, Professor Rick Lints of Gordon-Conwell Seminary, is far more helpful when he states, 'The central issue in the Second Commandment is idolatry, which may have to do with concrete images of God, but may not. Idolatry is worshipping an aspect of creation as if it were the Creator. However, I do not think the concreteness of the visual image (movie) is itself a violation of the Second Commandment. After all, Jesus is in fact, the image of God — and therefore already "concrete".' This is a biblical view I share and applaud. For if the VanDrunen view is right, then one wonders where was the outrage when films such as *Jesus of Nazareth*, or even *Ben Hur*, both of which also depicted Christ (albeit in the background in Ben Hur), were released? The fact is that barely anyone from the Bible-believing community bothered to level the charge against those films and those filmmakers. Whatever biblical charge may be levelled against Gibson's film, the breaking of the Second Commandment (and thereby the idolatry associated with that charge) ought not to be one of them.

With the chief indictment from most demurring evangelicals now removed, it is in Rick Lints' final remarks that we also gain a better insight into the whole issue. He states: 'Finally I would add that I am going to see it to be able to participate in the cultural conversation about the movie. In the same vein, I might visit a Roman Catholic cathedral in order to understand better the view of Christian faith which it exhibits, without thereby sanctioning the cathedral as the "biblical view of architecture" or some such thing...as a "cultural visitor", it would be entirely appropriate, I think.' This was the same reasoning I employed in going to see the film during the opening week in the UK. And there is a biblical mandate for such an approach which reveals that even significant religious matters can assume a 'cultural aspect' for believers.

The prophet Elisha had just healed Naaman's leprosy (2 Kings 5) when Naaman made an unusual 'cultural' request. He requested that he be might allowed to attend ceremonies involving the worship of a false god! He asks Elisha:

> Yet in this thing may the Lord pardon your servant: when my master [the King of Syria] goes into the temple of Rimmon to worship there, and he leans on my hand, and I bow down in the temple of Rimmon — when I bow down in the temple of Rimmon, may the Lord please pardon your servant in this thing (v.18).

What I think is going on occasionally when Christianity and 'secular' culture 'interface' is not always clearcut and irreligious. It can depend to an extent on the mind and understanding of the participant. For the sake of the 'weaker conscience' of some brethren, it may be that the more strong-minded should forgo their liberty for the sake of others, though they themselves may not be tainted or affected in any way. In the case of the apparently strong-minded Naaman, Elisha clearly saw no problem, answering him with an affirmative: 'Go in peace' (v.19). Now Naaman, as part of his duties, had little alternative other than to attend these ceremonies with his king. In this Elisha made no attempt to deter him. As Rick Lints points out, we might well become an observer at a Roman Catholic mass without being an active participant. Here we are dealing with a mere film and not with any worship activity. However, if we come away seeing it in exalted, overblown Christian terms, when, by its very nature, it lacks *thorough* biblical integrity, we may well be guilty of revealing a lack of spiritual discernment. The danger of that could easily be that we fall into sin, or are responsible for others doing so by our casual attitude or comments. It is this which should concern us, not whether the film is biblically faithful in its less important aspects. How could it be?

There is always a tension for Christians, as we have seen, by being 'in the world, but not of it'. The world cares nothing for holiness, either its own or ours. Living out this tension in practice will always mean facing and discerning the need to choose between 'keeping ourselves spotless from the world' and playing a full role in social and community life and affairs. It is the difficulties associated with this tension that caused our Reformational theologians to be so diverse in their assessment. Neither were they able to agree (and indeed took opposing views) on what was a key issue, such as the breaking of the Second Commandment. In the absence then of plain, core theological condemnations, perhaps we should realize that the more nuanced approach is to be preferred. Or let us put it another way. If for some, their consciences dictate that the film is or may be in some way blasphemous 'to them', then they should not see it. If, however, for others, it does not bear the marks of blasphemy and has a 'cultural' perspective (seeing it as Christian art or for the benefit of others) then that too is biblically valid.

The tension between personal pietism v. concern for communal welfare

In the case of the Gibson film, this writer agrees with the contention of Rick Lints, that Christians are free to take either approach *in this particular case*, viewing it or not according to their sanctified consciences. And this will have a knock-on effect for those whom we might decide to take with us to see it. It will also be necessary, in view of the film's screen violence, to assess whether those we take (or view with) are of a sensitive nature or perhaps well used to seeing on-screen violence. One of the things which struck me about the film was the 'manly' nature of the Jesus portrayed in it. I have no problem with this at all. It is a 'manliness' that *is* reflected in the Scriptures — a far cry from the insipid and fey portrayal of so many modern Christian books (which seems to bother very few critics!). This approach will, I have no doubt, affect many non-Christian men, as appears borne out (see below) by the evidence to date.

The film has taken artistic licence. It has included scenes which some of us would have left out for the sake of accuracy. But if it 'has put some off Christ', as some claim, one wonders at the large numbers, the two thousand-plus, who contacted the Christian Enquiry Agency for help and information after seeing the film in the first few weeks of it opening in the UK; the range of positive acclaim by secular critics;[3] and the reporting of countless stories of murderers and other felons turning to Christ and 'giving themselves up to justice',[4] especially in the USA. One wonders also at the number of Muslims who reportedly have flocked to see the film in countries such as Qatar and Brunei, stunned by a Christ who speaks in the familiar Aramaic language, and who have gone on to request Bibles in Aramaic.[5]

There are, however, some reservations which should not be dismissed out of hand. One or two of the contributors in the *MR* debate spoke of the power of the visual image, and how such images can easily 'roll around':literally, how some images dominate in the minds of some, subverting the biblical 'image', for instance, when it comes to the partaking of the Lord's Supper. This is a valid point. Once again, the issue of impressionable minds is raised. There is no doubt that some found the film a profoundly powerful and moving experience and, in certain cases, personal experience counts for more than biblical truth. But the Bible itself recognizes this 'easily influenced' syndrome and has a remedy for it. When it comes to the 'cultural' issue of drink, for instance, while pointing out to the mature Christian that 'for the sake of the conscience of weaker brethren' (1 Cor.8:12) they may be required to forgo their personal freedom to imbibe alcoholic drink (or eat meat offered to idols for that matter), the caveat should not be read as a blanket instruction to all Christians for abstinence on all occasions, especially those of a 'stronger mind'. Indeed, to take the argument that far is simply to commit another sin, the sin of legalism. My fear is that some evangelical detractors, who have issued blanket condemnations of this particular film, are presumptuously going beyond Scripture and, inadvertently, falling into this trap.

The same is true, I believe, with many cultural matters and 'influences' (including a book or film which relates the gospel story — especially one as graphically violent as Gibson's). Its images could indeed be likely to 'roll around' in some minds for long after the final reel has spun. Having said that, the images from Gibson's film lasted no more than a day or so with me, as with many who saw it. In fact, having seen the film on a Monday, the images did not even survive with me until the following Sunday (and we gather around the Lord's Table weekly)!

The Passion as 'Christian' art
The people whom the film really seems to have upset are those who do not understand what it actually means to be 'anti-Semitic'; those who hate to see Christ and the Christian faith in a positive light; those who baulk at the graphic depiction of violence (either because they deem it gratuitous or

simply because they don't want to see it); those Christians who do not understand what the Second Commandment actually prohibits; and other Christians who have written it off because the film went beyond Scripture.

Once again we are faced with the fact that it was made from the perspective of a man of a sect of Romanism, when that church has, since medieval times, never taken a Scripture-only approach to what it deems as truth. But we must keep in mind that there are two distinct things here. First, there are Gibson's personal motives for making it, particularly his assertions that it provides an excellent evangelistic opportunity. Second, there is the film in its own 'cultural' right. Most people who see it will have no knowledge of Gibson's motives, biblical or otherwise. So how then does it stand up to scrutiny in its cultural setting, but from a biblical worldview?

We have already seen that, as with other depictions of Jesus (and the historical fact of his actual physical, visual presence here among us), infringement of the Second Commandment is ruled out. Other objections surround extra-biblical material and a Roman Catholic slant. This includes, in the first case, the nonsense of a crow pecking out the eye of the aggressive one of the two who died with Christ at the Cross. It includes Judas being tormented by devils; the devil wafting unseen in and out of crowds; and tempting Christ in the garden (though some would say merely *suggesting* something of the devil's role in biblical events). And, as regards the second objection, an emphasis on Mary's role. But Mary would indeed have been 'somewhere', doing 'something'. These extra-biblical insertions, in my view mere moments here and there, do nothing to divert or detract from the main theme of the film's basically biblical account (at least in all its essentials).

Without question all of this extra-biblical material calls into question whether the film should be perceived as an 'excellent evangelism opportunity' by Christians. In this sense, claims that it is the best evangelistic opportunity 'ever' are simply absurd. But so too is the claim at the opposite end of the spectrum that the film should be condemned as blasphemous or idolatrous. As T. David Gordon, a theological professor in Grove City, Pennsylvania (a contributor to the *MR* forum above) put it, 'I don't intend to see Gibson's film, but I'm not launching a campaign against it either. Having lived through *Godspell* and *Jesus Christ Superstar*, I doubt that the film will either aid or injure the cause of Christianity significantly'. If, as we have seen, leading Reformational pastor/theologians (seven in the case of the *MR* forum), those whom we might trust most to be able to apply the Scriptures, *cannot* provide us with any perfectly plain biblical reasons why the film is to be avoided for Christians or for Christian evangelism, then, with the caveat that those of a more sensitive disposition should perhaps not see it, neither should we be quick to pass judgment.

When Martin Scorcese's production of *The Last Temptation of Christ* was released, with its highly publicized depiction of Jesus and Mary Magdalene engaged in a sexual relationship, the whole church knew, without seeing the film, that it was offensive and blasphemous. In such circumstances where the sinless Christ is depicted as having a sinful nature, the whole church should condemn it and avoid it. Such a book or film we are called to avoid personally, warn against loudly, and condemn vociferously as attacking the attributes of God.

But, as the *MR* forum plainly shows, neither heresy nor blasphemy marks Gibson's *The Passion*. Though there *are* extra-biblical interpretations and insertions, they are no more than incidental in what is otherwise a fairly Bible-inspired production in terms of its central themes, adherence to critical doctrine, and its thoroughly positive portrayal of Christ and the Christian faith. Could we possibly say the same about the wealth of Christian books being published in our day?

Conclusion

It would perhaps be as well if we in the church and Christians generally were to recover the gift of spiritual discernment, which will mean applying the Scriptures carefully in areas where faith and culture interact. To do so we shall need to relearn that secular culture is not necessarily to be feared. That God, by his common grace, has given to us many gifts, including the gift of film. Evangelicals, at one end of the spectrum, have shamefully imbibed all that culture has to offer, merely 'christianizing' it. At the other end of the spectrum, many have withdrawn from the culture altogether into a 'holy-huddle' fearfulness, seeing all modern culture as essentially secular and non-Christian. Between these two extremes there appears to be little or no recognition of a very broad cusp where God has given us his ordinary and common gifts to enjoy in culture.

Whether we see *The Passion of the Christ*, or indeed any film, book, painting, song or artful depiction of Christ as making for good or bad evangelism, the reality of its cultural, non-blasphemous, presence among us is plain enough. There will be times, as with Scorsese's *The Last Temptation of Christ*, that we must cry foul and condemn it out of hand. But in other cases, whether we view it as great evangelism or not, we can perhaps learn as much about the subject matter as we can (even taking the trouble to go and see it!) and use it as perfectly valid cultural *pre*-evangelism.

In such a situation this writer concurs with the view of Rick Lints, who clearly saw the higher need, in the absence of any overt serious reason to condemn, to see the film as a church leader, before congregants did and so that he might properly engage in the cultural debate. As with Lint, I saw the film, not because I particularly wanted to or had any real interest (I had to find the time to go), but rather as a church leader whose highest concern is for the sanctity and health of the church and congregants in our own church.

It is a difficult balance. But I have always taken the view that my own personal piety is not to be considered more highly than my service of Christ's church. After the event, of course, I find that I am not only more likely to know what I am talking about (and recognize serious flaws in the arguments of detractors, to boot), but also am better equipped to introduce non-believers who have seen it. To take them from Gibson's private 'take', to the only 'take' on Christ that really matters: the scriptural account.

---

[1] This a fact that some evangelical detractors of the film appear to have missed — see Mary's rhetorically whispered question to a distant Jesus: 'How long will *you* allow this to go on?' This may not be a direct biblical quote. But what evangelical detractors should note is that it *does* speak volumes in terms of right theology.

[2] Since the issue mentioned was published, *Modern Reformation* magazine has become independent of the Alliance of Confessing Evangelicals.

[3] Reported in the US Christian magazine *World*, 10 April 2004, p.13.

[4] Numerous newspaper reports, including news article *World* magazine, 10 April 2004, p.10.

[5] Reported in the *Evangelical Times*, May 2004, p.2.

ISSUES: the modern Christian mind

11
Why Are So Many Modern Christians *So* Gullible?

A plea for a return to confessional standards that Christians everywhere may know what the church, and they, believe

There is no question about it. We have got to stop thinking of liberals in the church as the nominal pew-fodder of long-declining Protestant denominations. These days, liberals come in all sorts of evangelical shapes and sizes. Indeed, given the fractured nature and disparate teachings of the Protestant and evangelical churches[1] at the beginning of the twenty-first century, our jumping-off point *ought* to be that these titles are today so devoid of meaning and cogent identity — by reason of the common abandonment of confessional standards — that they offer no real consensus catholic worldview[2] or sense of unity, either to their own members or to the surrounding culture.

Above all, what this has achieved is the loss of any semblance of that 'oneness' which the Bible itself *demands* (see Ephesians 4), rendering any talk of a comprehensive pattern of belief in a proper *biblical worldview* incomprehensible to both its own members and to non-believers alike, as well as, therefore, irrelevant in the world.

Why the label 'Bible-believing' is just not good enough
This is not to say that large numbers in the evangelical world do not labour to assert themselves as 'Bible-believing' (synonymous with what 'evangelical' *used* to mean). In practice, however, that title invariably reveals nothing more than an independently devised, often sectarian, privatized belief system, where 'Bible-believing' means 'whatever I say it means' and not what the historic consensus of the church has always said it means.[3]

The average evangelical believer today is simply 'tossed to and fro and carried about with every wind of doctrine' (Eph. 4:14), clueless as to the consistent biblical pattern of belief held by them or their church, let alone within a creed which they could articulate. But with the current crisis of leadership in our pulpits, poor teaching has simply aided and abetted the inherent gullibility of individual evangelicals in matters doctrinal, with countless numbers now simply forced to rely increasingly on the 'supplements' on offer from the burgeoning parachurch industry, with its own variety of quick-fix answers.

The result is that we have an increasingly schismatic climate within Protestant evangelicalism, with leading commentators already hearing our movement's 'death rattle'.[4] Commenting on the fact of the evangelical plunge into 'astounding theological illiteracy'[5], David Wells notes that 'The heretics of old, one suspects, would be sick with envy if they knew of the easy pickings that can now be had in the church'.[6] How right he is. It is as if we evangelicals have all taken to various lifeboats, only to drift in different directions on a sea of turbulent cultural waves and violent theological crosscurrents — wholly failing to notice our mother ship quietly slipping beneath the waves in the background.

But who helped to sink the ship?

For over one hundred years, between 1850 and 1950, the results of the relentless attack by the liberal enlightenment on the authority of the Bible led to countless 'Christian' cults springing up. The reason that Mormons, Jehovah's Witnesses and others could call themselves Christians at all was that they each could make the claim to being *the* 'Bible-believing' church. This has always been the way, as Peter pointed out, with those who 'untaught and unstable, twist [the Scriptures] to their own destruction' (2 Pet.3:16). This is *precisely* why Peter makes the point that the private interpretation of Scripture is taken *out of the hands of individuals* and placed in the hand of the consensus mind of the whole people of God, the historic church (2 Pet. 1:20), echoing the foundational teaching on the subject at Genesis 40:8.

In previous centuries the church could simply turn to its pattern of apostolic teaching, brought into more easily digestible form in the ecumenical confessions and creeds of the church catholic, to identify with ease whether some new teaching was the teaching of the true church or not. In this way the expansive, biblically-rooted ecumenical confessions of the church proved to be essential bulwarks guarding church 'oneness'. The Protestant Reformers themselves not only acknowledged this fully, but also laboured themselves to protect this same understanding for the sake of the church by restating eternal truths in expansive Reformation confessions as a *de facto* recognition of the *only* serious manner by which genuine unity could be achieved and meaningful.

Not for them the gushing shows of 'love' and vague claims to privatized 'Bible-believing' status, by which the Christian cults and the modern neo-evangelical churches now attract their members.[7] Today, however, we find countless Protestant and evangelical groups attempting to pursue unity, not by the historic church and Reformation basis of detailed confessional standards, but by adopting the unqualified label

'Bible-believing'. This usually means a chiselled-down rump of what they believe are 'essentials' which relate to how we are justified, but which provide not a jot of information about the manner in which we are sanctified and grown to maturity — the main work! Whilst it would be folly to deny that some doctrines are more important than others, it would be equal folly to deny that Scripture nowhere provides for the church catholic to teach anything less than the *'form of doctrine* to which you have been delivered' (Rom. 6:17) and to 'hold fast that pattern of sound words which you have heard from me' (2 Tim. 1:13).

It is asserted plainly here that 'cheapened' pragmatic unities based on 'the essentials', or even (C.S. Lewis's) 'mere Christianity', or even on the footing of a vacuous 'Bible-believing' tag, not only possess *no* biblical mandate, but are actual impediments to the biblical vision for true unity. Added to this is the theological idiocy of those bringing their own personal (modern) shibboleths to the process as 'badges of orthodoxy' — such as the cultic King James Only Version and (singing) Psalms-only cultist sectarians who are only factionalizing the church still further.

Cult-like belief and practice invade the evangelical church, too

By the middle of the twentieth century, even though liberal modernism ran out of intellectual steam, such was the damage inflicted upon the Protestant psyche that confidence in the power of the Word of God no longer meant what it once did. As postmodernism came in, with its 'whatever is true for you *is* true' ethic, many perceived a 'better chance' for the Christian message. But just as the greater danger in world religions is the Hindu 'all systems are true' ethic (and *not,* as is widely perceived, the monotheistic Islamic system), so too the dangers of postmodernism proved just as deadly to the true gospel as modernism. With the rise of postmodernism, the scene was now set for a further dramatic fracturing of the church consensus, this time over decades rather than centuries.

With the barrier of confessionalism increasingly a thing of the past, many local churches have now been thrown back upon their 'own understanding'. Some have bravely held out (and still do) for their confessional standards. But they are a depressingly small number; with far more seemingly content to proceed on the non-articulating 'Bible-believing' banner, as if this were anything other than a postmodern expression, one which means whatever anyone wants it to mean. The result has been the loss of the 'pattern of sound words' delivered by the prophets and the apostles.

Perhaps we can see, in retrospect, just how easy we have made it for a whole *new* evangelicalism, with its private baggage of unbiblical beliefs and practices, to set up their market stalls within the precincts of the evangelical 'temple'. And yet, if like Jesus we were to take a moment to know our own verbal 'cord of knots' by reference to our biblical and confessional standards, we could easily drive out the whole smorgasboard of the Word-Faith movement, seeker-sensitive man-focused worship, new prophetic revelation movements, and countless other non-biblical belief movements at a stroke.

A simplistic pipedream? Perhaps, but it *is* a thoroughly biblically-mandated one. One thing is certain. Without a return to confessional standards of belief and practice we can kiss goodbye to any serious prospect of achieving the only unity mandated by Scripture. And in such a climate, is it any wonder that the contemporary Christian, at the beginning of the twenty-first century, is wandering around in something of a spiritual haze; not really *understanding* the full-orbed logicality of their faith; and completely at sea in terms of applying it to the real world? Is it any surprise that the world considers the modern church and the Christian as both theologically and culturally incoherent?

A plea for a return to confessionalism

When today we ask why Christians are making so many mistakes in gullibly accepting non-biblical beliefs and practices, the short answer is that, because so many are so badly taught by teachers who themselves have no concept of holding fast to the pattern of sound words delivered to them, they will look to anything which appears to be effectual (pragmaticism). As a result many modern Christians have little or no idea what it means to be spiritual at all. They conceive of being spiritual as something esoteric, indefinable, piestistic and private. The Bible teaches no such spirituality. It defines true spirituality as, 'draw[ing] near with a true heart' (Heb. 10:22) to God and his Word. This is manifested by three marks: a) 'holding fast the confession of our hope' (v.23) — i.e. the internal receiving of the pattern of sound words; b) 'consider[ing] one another in order to stir up good works' (v.24) — the practical outworking of our faith; and c) 'not forsaking the assembling of ourselves together' (v.25) — the much undervalued doctrine of church and all that it means biblically. *Note:* only one of these is *internal* (genuine pietism as a Word-motivated heart and mind), while the other two are *external* — fully exposing the deficiencies of the modern evangelical mind and understanding concerning the importance of external, church *'catholic'* matters.

If there is to be any hope for the future of evangelicalism, we need to repent of the unbiblical privatization of faith by our cultural abandonment of the unifying confessional standards of faith. If we are to be able to reform the fractured body of Christ's church once again, then we must not leave the individual church members and individual churches floundering, fighting theological and cultural skirmishes in isolation, when the real battle *ought* to belong to the whole army — the church itself.

---

[1] 'Autonomous local franchises' would perhaps be a more accurate description.

[2] Unless stated to the contrary, 'catholic' here means 'universal' and not 'Roman Catholic'.

[3] This is born out by the frightening results of recent surveys of Christian beliefs. In a survey by George Barna's evangelical research group in the USA, 26 per cent of all evangelicals believe that all religions are basically the same; 50 per cent of evangelicals believe that a life of good works will get people to heaven; and 35 per cent of 'born again' evangelicals do not believe Jesus ever rose physically from the dead. As the commenting article title made clear, this means that many evangelicals today are actually unbelievers. Statistics taken from 'Unbelieving "born-agains": Research continues to reveal a steady theological collapse among professing Christians in America' by Gene Veith, *Word* magazine, 6 Dec. 2003, p. 33.

[4] David Wells, *No Place for Truth: Or Whatever Happened to Evangelical Theology:* (Grand Rapids, MI: Eerdmans, 1993), p.134.

[5] ibid., p.4.

[6] ibid., p.183.

[7] Who in their right mind would *want* to join a cult? It is overt practical expressions of love and biblical fidelity which prove alluring.

ISSUE: the nature of Christian worship
& who defines it

12
The Church in Cyberspace
Going where no church has gone before?

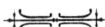

Given its decline in our generation, worldly cynics might observe that the modern church needs 'all the help it can get'. Along with liberals in the church itself, they might then be incredulous to learn that many Christians view the attempt to 'be church' and 'do worship' in cyberspace, as just another doomed attempt aimed at turning the tide of spiritual decay. The truth is, however, quite different. What the church needs is God's help *to obey God's agenda for it* — no more, no less. And what that would mean is a recovery of the biblical understanding of what it means to be church in the first place.

The worldwide web certainly has a place in supporting the general work of the Christian church. But when it comes to setting up a virtual church community in cyberspace, as part of the latest communications revolution, then the surfer can no more be a member of a legitimate 'church' than the reader could via the printing press.

Where no church has gone before

In the spring of 2004 the first two web-based church worship services went public in the UK. They were the Church of England's 'I-Church', based in the Oxford diocese, and the Methodist-sponsored 'Church of Fools', a project of the Ship of Fools online Christian magazine. Those behind these two media events admit 'uncertainty' as pioneers in their new enterprises. The 'Church of Fools' website even states that it chose its title to be seen to be 'poking fun' at itself. Now as anyone who knows me will testify, I am not averse to utilizing humour to make a point. But I would find it difficult to garner from Scripture a mandate for a church of Christ to ridicule itself and refuse to take seriously its role as a worshipping community.

The 'Church of Fools' founders state that it is not their intention to overthrow 'real' church. But equally they make it clear that they do believe that 'the net offers people the chance for genuine meetings and true community', that the cyberchurch can, prospectively, legitimately take its place alongside the 'real' church. And this begs two very different and key questions. Is a 'community' in cyberspace a legitimate extension of the corporate body of Christ on earth? Or is it rather yet further proof that many modern Christians have no biblical understanding at all of what it means to be 'church'? In addition, it is perhaps noteworthy that these same two innovative online 'churches' were sponsored by two of the fastest-declining denominations in the UK[1] — denominations actively searching for 'new ideas' to stem the deterioration.

Fools for Christ — or a church of fools?

The title 'Church of Fools'[2] is no doubt a self-deprecating allusion to the apostle Paul's 'fools for Christ' reference at 1 Corinthians 4:10. In that passage the great apostle speaks of the need to become 'fools for Christ'. The context of his argument is that the world views the beliefs and practices of the Christian church as 'foolishness'. What the passage does not suggest, however, is that Christians should be 'fools' in any other sense. What then are we to make of Christians who believe it is perfectly possible to hold 'genuine meetings' and experience 'true community' via screens and wires?

Now let me be clear what I am NOT saying here. I am not saying that the Internet is no place for the modern church in the broader non-worshipping sense — far from it. I have long been an advocate of Christians and the church getting involved in every aspect of Internet communication, when it comes to the furtherance of the gospel and Christian teaching. Where the Christian message is systematically being stifled in the liberal-dominated media world — and increasingly in the world of print publishing — the web presents the church with a veritable cyberspace Areopagus, an unfettered voice in the free marketplace of ideas. Indeed, we would be right to welcome the freedom which the Internet provides for the proclamation of the gospel by echoing the sentiments of Samuel Morse who, sending the very first electric telegraph, tapped out joyously: 'What hath God wrought!' (Numbers 23:23).

But, while the presence of Christian evangelism, support information and all manner of other church-Net support is fine, there can be no alternative to the reality of sharing and worshipping in a common understanding of the faith in a local community. The fact that some modern church leaders have come to believe it is possible to do so, that cyberchurch or cyberworship in virtual 'communion' with a ragbag of unknown individuals (who may well hold no catholic truths in common at all!), dispensing entirely with the sacrament of 'breaking bread' at a common table,[3] provides yet a further cause for spiritual concern in the modern church. How 'on earth', we should want to know, is the church eldership to maintain the sanctity and health of common church life, including the pastoring and disciplining of the flock? Perhaps by a Star Trek-like 'beaming' here and there to various far-flung locations? All this brings into sharp focus the God-given, apostolic teaching and biblical mandate that defines what it means to be church.

When is a church 'a church'?
There is no way in this short article that I can do full justice to what it means to be 'church' in every age until Christ returns. But it is clear, not least through the setting up of these two virtual cybercommunities as 'true churches', that increasing numbers of Christians are today so biblically uninformed that they no longer know what it means to be church. As I point out in my book The Virtual Church and How to Avoid It, the cyberchurch, in terms of its virtual imitation of a true church as defined in Scripture, is nothing less than a spiritual 'dead duck'.

To begin with, the three Bible-authorizing elements that make a church 'a church' in God's (not man's) sight are: the faithful preaching of the Word (John 8:31,47; Gal.1:8-9; 2 Thess.2:15; 2 Tim.3:16-4:4; 1 John 4:1-3); the right administration of the sacraments (1 Cor. 10:14-17,21; 1 Cor. 11:23-30); and the exercise of church discipline, as required by the first two (Matt.18:17; Acts 20:28-31; Rom. 16:17-18; 1 Cor. 5:1-13). It does not take long to work out that the first of these three has already become victim of modern practice in churches generally (and is the *real* root of *all* our church woes today!), never mind on the web. The great sadness of our generation is that Bible-believing Christians are finding faithful churches increasingly scarce. And though the preaching of the Word can occur online, the Bible makes it clear that that preaching ought primarily to be within the context of community church life, not apart from it. But the other two elements, sacrament observance, and the pastoring and disciplining of the flock, are simply impossible to administer there. It should be plain to the thinking Christian that God himself has instituted the universal (catholic) Christian church and deems communal catholicity within local communities the best expression of that faith.

We need to ask ourselves: how can we get to know one another and pray for each other's needs if we do not have genuine interactive fellowship over a period of time, with the same people visiting each other's homes, getting to know one another's families and friends? How can we claim to hold belief and practice in common if we do not know what we believe confessionally, as one, 'as church'? And are we not giving up a primary conduit for receiving God's grace if we abandon the practice of the Lord's Supper which Christ himself instituted?

The truth is (and our generation has been particularly guilty of this) that many churches, including evangelical churches, have come to view the Lord's Supper as entirely superfluous to true church worship. And yet, at 1 Corinthians 11, Paul is at pains to point out that those who abuse the Supper may well fall ill — with some even dying (vs.30). Such is the importance of it at the heart of all church life! And the prospect of administering church discipline, the natural and necessary corollary of safeguarding the sanctity and health of the church community — which goes hand in hand with attendance at the Lord's Table — becomes a total non-starter in cyberspace.

Back on Planet Earth

Though the Christian church has many things to offer and teach the world as well as individual Christians via the worldwide web, the reality of meaningful church membership, and thereby genuine community church worship, is not one of them. If we are to rediscover precisely what it means to be church, then we ought humbly to admit that God actively seeks those who desire to worship him in 'spirit and truth' (John 4:23,24). Sincerity *alone* in church and worship is not enough. 'What *is* truth?' asked Pilate. 'Your Word is truth,' says Jesus. Thus, Christ teaches that *all* worship (and worship *is* the heart of all church life) is defined biblically, not by the whims of men's perhaps sincere, but ultimately futile, agenda.

If we are to be restored to a more fruitful relationship with God, what the modern church must understand is that culture generally has forgotten the concept of meaningful community, and the modern church is following suit. We can only exacerbate the situation if we settle for a virtual reality, customized version of church 'down a tube'. One key element of Christian witness (and perhaps the only one many express at all) is the absurd and puzzling practice (as our neighbours, friends and families see it) of getting up Sunday by Sunday and joining with other believers in a joint and highly public act of community witness for Christ. If we routinely exempt ourselves from that weekly Sabbath act, preferring to pursue individual, isolated 'communion'[4] with a geographically dispersed and depersonalized 'church', we shall quickly find ourselves in the area of offering God presumptuous, profane (unauthorized) and, ultimately, unacceptable worship. God has made known his 'non-negotiables' which mark a church as a true church. For, when all is said and done, 'a church' is what God says it is, not what we conceive it to be.

So if we are considering the option of joining the cyber-church revolution, we must ask ourselves: do we want to be members of a virtual-reality church powered courtesy of the electricity companies; or a true church, authorized and empowered by Christ?

---

[1] As I have written elsewhere, one of the Anglican Church's own internal reports has described the Church of England as 'in meltdown', while

the Methodist Church (I happen to live in a converted Methodist Chapel and my local Presbyterian church now lodges in another) has been in terminal decay for many years.

[2] Linked, as it is, with the often (in other more positive ways) humorous online *Ship of Fools* website.

[3] See Acts 2:42, which sets out the essential elements for all main Sabbath church meetings.

[4] Such an oxymoron speaks volumes! Divinely acceptable worship requires a very real congregation meeting in one physical location (Acts 2:44; 1 Cor. 11:18,20a).

By the same author

The Virtual Church - and how to avoid it
The Crisis of De-formation and the Need for Re-formation in the 21st Century Church (Xulon Press ISBN 1 594673 98 5)

For further copies of this book in the USA
ring the toll free orderline at Xulon Press, Florida
1-866-381-2665 ext.109
or email: bookorder-xp@xulonpress.com

(All Xulon Press titles are also distributed by Ingram and Spring Arbour Book Distributors in the USA)

For orders in the UK & Europe
ring the orderline or fax UK distributor **Word21** on 01206 231138
or email: orders@word21.com
or visit: www.word21.com

Word21 for the very best conservative and Christian books and resources

NB. The usual discounts are available for retailers and libraries.

All titles can also be ordered through Amazon online, Barnes and Noble and from all normal retail outlets.

Author Biography

Peter C Glover is director of Word21 (see www.word21.com), which produces conservative and Christian books and resources dealing with contemporary political, social, cultural and faith issues. He is author of *The Virtual Church* and *The Politics of Faith* (Xulon Press).

In the 1980s and 90s he worked in the law and as a national spokesman for the Director of Public Prosecutions/ Crown Prosecution Service national HQ and for an international HIV/AIDS charity. For eight years, until early 2004, he was director of the Christian Research Network (CRN) researching contemporary religious movements and cults, during which time he also edited and contributed to the *CRN Journal*.

He conceived, contributed to, and edited, the bestselling *Signs & Wonders Movement Exposed* (Day One Publications) and has had numerous articles on cultural, social political and church issues published over many years.

He currently works as a freelance media consultant & writer and is part-time associate pastor of Emmanuel Presbyterian Church in Clacton, Essex. He is married to Sara and they live in a converted chapel near Colchester. Both love music, walking and playing squash.

Printed in the United Kingdom
by Lightning Source UK Ltd.
102049UKS00001B/172-408